The Ballad of Jacob Peck

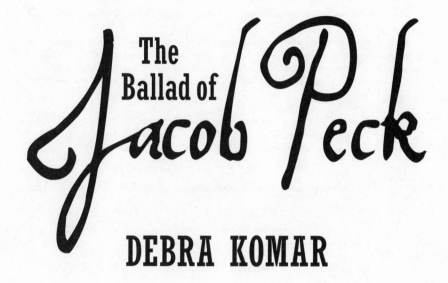

The Ballad of Jacob Peck

DEBRA KOMAR

GOOSE LANE

Edited by Barry Norris.
Cover image: Thomas Tolkien (http://thomastolkien.wordpress.com)
Cover design and page design by Chris Tompkins and Julie Scriver.

Library and Archives Canada Cataloguing in Publication

Komar, Debra, 1965-
The ballad of Jacob Peck / Debra Komar.
Includes bibliographical references and index.
Also issued in electronic format.
ISBN 978-0-86492-903-7

1. Peck, Jacob. 2. Babcock, Amos. 3. Hall, Mercy.
4. Murder—New Brunswick—History—19th century.
5. Circuit riders—New Brunswick—Biography. I. Title.

HV6535.C32N42 2013   364.152'3097151   C2012-907145-5

Goose Lane Editions acknowledges the generous support of the Canada Council for the Arts, the Government of Canada through the Canada Book Fund (CBF), and the Government of New Brunswick through the Department of Tourism, Heritage, and Culture.

Goose Lane Editions
500 Beaverbrook Court, Suite 330
Fredericton, New Brunswick
CANADA E3B 5X4
www.gooselane.com

To Sarah Lathrop and Steph Davy-Jow,
true and wondrous friends,
for never once suggesting
that I keep my day job.

The Ballad of Jacob Peck

Amasa Babcock lived in a shack outside of Shediac, New Brunswick
He had a wife and nine children and a sister of melancholy disposition
She was not able to come to the table

Jacob Peck arrived in the cold winter of 1805
He was an expert crowd rouser, in an era of hellfire preachers
He'd whip you into a frenzy at his mad house revival parties

Jacob Peck, he put a rope around Babcock's neck
Put him in a trance, some kind of zombie romance
The hypnotic rant of a hellfire preacher
Hellfire, Hellfire

Babcock held up a handful of grain from his hand mill
Removed his boots and socks revealing
"this is the bread of heaven, the stars are falling"
The whole family went nuts as they backed up against the bench
Babcock drew a knife and sharpened it, set his strength to kill his sister
with it
And in the bloody mayhem, everybody snapped to their senses

Babcock ended up in a Dorchester jail
He had nobody to defend him
And the jury found him guilty and the judge sentenced him to hang
There was no compensation for an innocent man

Jacob Peck, he put a rope around Babcock's neck
Put him in a trance, some kind of zombie romance
The hypnotic rant of a hellfire preacher
Hellfire, Hellfire

One more for the hangman
Gloves for the hangman

John Bottomley, 1992
Reprinted with permission

Contents

Preface
In limine

Errors and misconceptions abound in the historical record. Personal opinion, speculation, and literary devices are introduced as fact and, if left unchallenged, become an accepted part of a legend. Far more elusive in the annals of history are those occasions when such errors can be traced back to an identifiable source. Yet, in the case of a gruesome murder that rocked an isolated settlement on New Brunswick's eastern shore in 1805, it is possible to pinpoint exactly how later accounts became littered with a startling array of fallacious details. Like the now-discredited theory of a mitochondrial Eve, myths disguised as truths regarding the murder were all born of a single source: an 1898 magazine article that inadvertently spawned generations of mutant versions of the tale.

The article, entitled "The Babcock Tragedy," was not the first public discourse of the case. Despite the sensational nature of the crime, its rural location and small English-speaking population allowed the story to escape the notice of all but one of the newspapers of the day. On June 26, 1805, the *Royal Gazette* published a brief summary of the murder trial, penned with bias by the prosecutor in the case — in the years before salaried news reporters, such was the fashion.

For almost eighty years, the case received little attention outside the confines of the tiny hamlet and erstwhile crime scene. Then, in 1884, scholar Joseph W. Lawrence revisited the murder in a lecture before the New Brunswick Historical Society, of which Lawrence was then president. Although no copies of his narrative survive in the public archives,[1] his talk revived interest in the case. In 1898, William Reynolds — writing under the pseudonym "Roslynde" — published his account of the tragedy in the inaugural issue of *New Brunswick Magazine*. The article was never externally vetted as Reynolds was also the magazine's editor and publisher. Reynolds's retelling of the story was rife with errors — from the name of the killer and other key players to the sequence of events surrounding the crime — yet, for want of scrutiny, it somehow became gospel.

In the years that followed, every published account of the crime has relied on the *New Brunswick* magazine article as its primary (and, in most cases, sole) source of information. Protracted discussions of the murder have been featured in a number of historical works, including Lawrence's posthumously published opus, *The Judges of New Brunswick and Their Times* (1915); *A History of Shediac, New Brunswick* by John Clarence Webster (1928); Fannie Chandler Bell's *A History of Old Shediac, New Brunswick* (1937); G.A. Rawlyk's *Ravished by the Spirit* (1984); and *Running Far In: The Story of Shediac* by John Belliveau (2003). The story has also received chapter-length treatments in popular crime anthologies, including B.J. Grant's *Six for the Hangman* (1983) and Allison Finnamore's *East Coast Murders: Mysteries, Crimes and Scandals* (2005), an account so bastardized it is best considered a work of fiction. In 1992 Canadian folksinger John Bottomley even set Grant's version to music; the lyrics of his haunting ballad introduce this book.

Without exception, the errors contained in Reynolds's 1898 article were propagated in each new rendition. Worse still, many authors took it upon themselves to embellish the story, offering their own unique twists and revisions to the tale. Like a child's game of "Telephone" played across the decades, the original message has morphed with each retelling, leaving the end result unrecognizable from the archetype. A lone academic consideration of the story by Professor David Graham Bell appeared as an appendix in his 1984 edited volume, *The Newlight Baptist Journals of James Manning and James Innis*.[2] His thesis focused on dispelling the oft-reported myth that one of the story's central characters — the itinerant preacher, Jacob Peck — was a Baptist, rather than a follower of the New Light movement. Though Bell's treatment far exceeds all prior accounts in terms of accuracy, often citing original historical documents, it is not without errors, as he too falls prey to embracing Reynolds's 1898 account as a reliable source.

If Bell's academic effort falls at one end of the credibility spectrum, with Reynolds and his followers occupying the middle ground, the lunatic fringe has laid claim to the far end, creating a Web-based fantasy realm populated by conspiracy theorists and ufologists. A particularly bizarre case in point: Paul Kimball,[3] a filmmaker who argues that a series of loud noises heard during one of Peck's more boisterous revivals was, in fact, proof of extraterrestrial visitation. To his credit, Kimball at least cites an original source in his quest to transform Amos Babcock — the ill-fated protagonist of the tragedy, convicted of butchering his sister — from murderer to alien abductee, lending a thin veneer of integrity to an otherwise ludicrous enterprise.

Misrepresentations and falsehoods notwithstanding, the crime is ineluctably worthy of the attention it has garnered over the years. Despite its garbled history, the tragic events in Shediac Parish during the winter of 1805 remain one of the most compelling and enduring murder cases in Canadian history. Set against the backdrop of a criminal justice system in its infancy and encompassing elements of madness, religious fervour, class warfare, and institutionalized bigotry among the English-speaking settlers and their Acadian and First Nations neighbours, the tale of Amos Babcock, Jacob Peck, and Mercy Hall is as salacious, controversial, and riveting today as it was more than two hundred years ago.

The tale warrants a proper telling for it remains a true murder mystery for the ages. In this case, the mystery lies not in whodunit — the person who wielded the murder weapon has never been a point of contention — but rather in a question that continues to haunt our legal system to this day: to what extent can one person be held accountable for the actions of another?

In a brave new digital world replete with recently defined crimes such as cyberbullying and wrongful deaths attributed to hostile Facebook posts, what are the legal consequences of speech and the actions it prompts? If I tell you to jump off a bridge and you do, am I legally culpable for your death, or would twelve jurors interpret such drastic action as a sign of mental instability? Where does one person's right to free speech end and another's responsibility for his or her own actions begin? Despite the judicial system's new-found dependency on high-tech forensic science, DNA cannot answer these complex moral and legal questions. That is why we have juries. It falls to every individual, and to society as a whole, to determine where we draw the line on personal responsibility. Although advances in digital social networking have renewed the debate, the question is centuries old. It was raised in a courthouse in New Brunswick in 1805, and the answers born of this landmark case resonate today. The modes of communication might have changed but the fundamental issue remains the same.

Errors in the historical record abound. So do gaps. Beginning with the 1898 article and cascading down through its muddled offspring, a single accusation reverberates: that the incendiary sermons of the preacher Jacob Peck directly contributed to the murder of Mercy Hall. In every iteration of the tale, the wagging finger of guilt is pointed squarely at the feckless cleric, yet not once in all those renditions do his accusers reveal what Peck supposedly said or did that spurred such violence, nor is it clear what crime they accuse Peck of committing. They are as certain of Peck's guilt as they are vague about his offence, providing a definitive answer to an unasked question.

An exhaustive search through the historical record, however, reveals the details of the "Babcock Tragedy." The picture that emerges answers the lingering question that is the focus of this investigation: should Jacob Peck have been charged in the murder of Mercy Hall and, if so, with what crime?

§

Preface **In limine**

This is a work of non-fiction. The characters are real, and all events are faithfully reconstructed from credible sources in the historical record. All text appearing within quotation marks is drawn from original materials: letters, journals, court records, autopsy reports, newspapers, and other documents. Legal procedures and standards are depicted and applied as they existed in 1805.

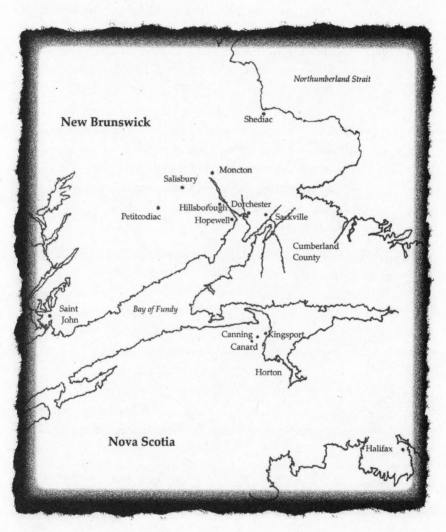

mens rea [law Latin, "a guilty mind"]
The requisite state of mind of the perpetrator
when committing the offence, revealing criminal
intent and an understanding that the action
violates the law.

Prologue

As Mercy's blood dripped onto the snow, a curious alchemy occurred. The fiery liquid punched a hole through the snow's crust and was tempered by the frozen layer beneath, even as the blood in turn caused it to melt. The result was an instantaneous exchange of energy, with a by-product reminiscent of the local yuletide confection made from boiling maple syrup poured onto a fresh bank of snow — viscous, malleable, and quickly consumed.

Mercy Hall's blood thickened and cooled, even as the worsening snow-fall erased the trail it marked. She was well past caring. She was now nothing more than dead weight, aptly named, on the shoulder of her brother Amos Babcock. In the waning moonlight, bolstered by the snow, the red blood read black. It soaked through Mercy's thin woollen dress and down the back of Amos's shirt and vest. Amos did not feel it, nor did he feel the cold. He sought only God's favour, although the Lord's blessing eluded Amos as well.

Drenched in blood and sweat, Amos forged on. In his hand he still held the knife. It too was coated in black. Slick with blood, it had twice slipped from his grasp. Without thought, Amos had wiped it against the coarse towelling he had tied around his waist.

In the distance, he heard muffled sobs emanating from his house. He turned, looking back. He had not travelled as far as he had hoped, burdened with Mercy's lifeless body, each footfall bound by a thick blanket of snow. The halo from the lone oil lamp barely escaped the house. There, silhouetted in the door frame, was the solemn figure of his wife, Dorcas. Dour and desolate, she marked Amos's progress as he fulfilled the task God had set, a task Amos vowed to complete.

Amos re-shouldered his burden. Only moments earlier, Amos's brother Jonathon had flung himself through that same doorway, lunging headfirst into the cold night air. Jonathon ran, manic, clutching the remnants of his clothes and struggling to pull on his boots as he staggered across the ice and snow. He fled toward the road, toward succour and sanity. The family's cabin lay a quarter-mile from their nearest neighbour. Even in the storm, Amos knew it would not be long before the others came.

Babcock turned back to the job at hand. He continued through the forest, away from the light and his wife's silent censure. He had no particular destination in mind but prayed for God to lead him to the chosen place. Forcing his way through a stand of pine, Amos surveyed the clearing. The wind had whipped the snow into crests, piling it high against the copse. Though he still could not hear the voice of God, Amos felt it was right.

With an indifference that would sicken his good Christian neighbours, Amos threw his sister's body into the deepest bank of snow. By now, little blood remained to seep from her wounds. Amos muttered a brief prayer, intelligible only to himself. He watched, immobile, as the snow began to cover Mercy's body.[1]

He could no longer feel his feet, bare against the ice, yet he stood transfixed. As the snow claimed Mercy's body, Amos turned and looked across the clearing, through the trees toward the house where his wife and nine children waited for him. Time was running out. The Rapture was at hand. God's message was clear; the preacher had been sent to deliver it. There was still work to be done.

In the coming months, there would be considerable debate as to Amos's mental state at this particular moment. Questions of sanity, religious fervour, and God's will would be raised in a court of law and in the court of public

Prologue

opinion. Whatever his current fettle, as Amos made his way back to the cabin, he had the presence of mind to cut a branch from a nearby pine and use the bough to sweep away his own footsteps in the freshly fallen snow.[2]

Act 1

Particeps criminis

res gestae [Latin, "things done"] The events in question.

The arrival

Jacob Peck [1]

In Shediac Parish, the arrival of Jacob Peck met with none of the hysteria that accompanied his departure some six weeks later. On that frigid morning — January 6, 1805 — his coming was neither expected nor welcome. His reputation had preceded him to the sparse settlers' enclave on New Brunswick's northeastern shore. He was known but not particularly respected. He had no family waiting, no acquaintance anxious for his company. He carried little in the way of luggage, preferring to travel light. He arrived prepared for a swift departure, should one prove necessary.

Peck's reputation — such as it was — was a volatile pastiche of the sacred and the profane. By profession he was a farmer, but by self-proclamation he was a preacher. His ministry was itinerant by design if not wholly by choice. He lacked proof of a formal education and was therefore ineligible for any permanent placement in a proper institution. In his quest to bring his message to the people, he was, at that moment, wending his way north from Moncton through the more negligible outlying settlements. In the parlance of the day, he was "working the circuit" — a well-trodden path forged by roaming evangelists who plied their trade in those communities lacking the benefit of organized religion. Peck's inclination was to arrive in a village, convert the willing few to his unique brand of theology, then attempt to establish a more enduring foothold. He had yet to succeed in that final step. Inevitably, within days of his arrival, Peck would beat a hasty retreat. Whether his departures were by choice or by community decree was grist for much speculation. As he slogged through the mire into the village, having made his way on foot for the past twenty miles, this was the sum total of what the good people of Shediac knew of the cryptic Mr. Peck.

For his part, Peck relished his notoriety. He enhanced his veiled image through secrecy. Little of his past was known for certain — his birthplace, education, previous employment, or even religious training — and this uncertainty suited him. Idle village gossip held that Peck was from the province's southern shore. Shediac town elder William Hanington later mistakenly identified Peck as hailing from "Potquodiach,"[2] a valiant effort at recalling the town of Petitcodiac, then as now a mere dot on the map to the southwest of the parish. Peck did little to correct any misconceptions others held of him, preferring the enticing aura of mystique to the dull safeguard of accuracy.

Whatever Peck's origins, his nature was of inexhaustible interest to his contemporaries. His Mephistophelean persona was both cultivated and consciously considered. When it suited him, Peck had the ability to charm, at least in the original meaning of the word: to cast a spell over the unwitting and easily beguiled. Endlessly (if falsely) self-effacing, he infiltrated a community through nuance and subtlety. Peck did not so much invade a new settlement as seep into it like a malignant fog.

Physically, Peck was an enigma. His exact age was indecipherable from his face, although many surmised he was in his fourth decade of life. His colouring belied his German heritage. He could accurately be called neither handsome nor plain, yet there was something in his face that compelled the viewer's attention. His eyes were piercing, a look considered hypnotic and commanding to some, challenging or even menacing to others. Although only of average height and slight build, his costume lent him a certain élan. Practicality, rather than the whims of fashion, dictated that a long coat remain the hallmark of the elite, but Peck made himself the exception, even if his reduced financial circumstances obliged him to wear the same trumped-up wardrobe year-round.

Peck's personality was equally contradictory. He openly craved attention, yet always sought the edges of a crowd. Save for the pulpit, he rarely called attention to himself, but held in an iron grip the gaze of those who engaged him. A testament to self-absorption, all of Peck's windows faced inward. He could be, by turns, winsome, craven, charismatic, reptilian, manipulative, untrustworthy, and a man of God. Despite his clerical facade, many of the townsfolk — chief among them William Hanington — thought Jacob Peck lacked integrity and a moral core.[3] As such, he could be many things to many people.

In all regards, Peck was a paradox. He was a profoundly vain man, yet he never commissioned a portrait or, in his later years, allowed his image to be captured in photographs. He fancied himself a scholar but resisted every entreaty to write down his learned words. He wielded a Bible at all times, both as a prop and a weapon, yet was never seen to open it.

There was little need. Peck's beliefs were not to be found within its pages. Jacob Peck professed to be a devotee of the New Light movement, a revivalist tradition that had taken hold among the English-speaking residents of the Maritimes.[4] In reality, Peck's biblical interpretations bore little resemblance to those of its founder, the Reverend Henry Alline.

During his lifetime, Alline proved highly controversial. He espoused universal salvation, arguing that although not all would be saved, all could be saved through baptism. Alline drew a hard line, railing against sins of the flesh and condemning drinking, horse racing, and other forms of worldly pleasure as "frolicking."[5] Still, his puritanical teachings struck a chord among settlers seeking a more dynamic yet temperate religious doctrine. His stern message outlasted his brief life. Henry Alline died in 1784 at the age of thirty-five. His tombstone bears the epitaph "the Apostle of Nova Scotia."[6]

In the years following his death, Alline's doctrine sparked the Second Great Awakening in Nova Scotia. The hellfire revival gained greater momentum as the century turned. Peck had ridden its popular coattails throughout neighbouring New Brunswick, but with his own unique spin on Alline's teachings. In the gospel according to Jacob Peck, salvation was not open to all but would be offered only to a select few, with Peck appointing himself arbiter. Peck also had no qualms about earthly pleasures, indulging in wanton "frolicking" whenever the opportunity arose. Rumours of his licentious nature only added to Peck's infamy.

By remaining in constant motion, Peck believed he could erase the sins of his past. At the very least, he could outrun them. But life as an itinerant preacher was not without drawbacks. Wandering through the wilds of New Brunswick in the dead of winter on foot had taken its toll. Peck was tired and was once again in need of a new congregation.

As Peck surveyed the streets of Shediac, his eyes landed on the very signs he sought. It was isolated and small, with fragile tethers to the outside world. The settlement lacked carriage or rail routes and had no established harbour. There were only three routes into the village: the one by land Peck himself had travelled and two others by sea. The Acadian population was twenty-two families, a hundred souls; the English settlers numbered half that.[7] Poverty was rampant, yet the telltale marks of affluence hinted at a class structure ripe for exploitation. Most important, the enclave had no church, no obvious centre of worship.[8]

With a cunning and instinct honed over years spent travelling the back roads of Acadia, Peck made his decision. He would rest awhile in this town and begin his ministry. He would save the souls of its inhabitants. On January 6, 1805 — without the residents' knowledge or consent — a New Light fell on Shediac Parish.

Another Awakening

In truth, Jacob Peck's life was a travesty, a pale spectre of the artful facade he presented to the denizens of Shediac Parish. His deft artifice was infinitely more compelling than his limited circumstance. Almost pathologically ashamed, he considered his humble birth and diminished social station handicaps to be vanquished, not through diligence but through deceit and misdirection.

Jacob Peck was born in 1765 in Cumberland County, Nova Scotia, on the rugged yet picturesque isthmus that links that province and New Brunswick. He was the third son and fourth child of Martin and Maria Peck. Father Martin was born in Germany in the final months of 1735, christened with the original family surname of Beck. At the tender age of sixteen, he and his older brother Michael joined a group of other German Protestants fleeing religious persecution or seeking freedom and fortune in the New World. In July 1751, *The Pearl*, captained by Thomas Francis, set sail from Rotterdam, bound for Halifax with 264 passengers on board.[2] Only 232 arrived: the rest were claimed by disease, dehydration, and the elements. Another casualty of the voyage was the surname Beck. As the ship docked, the brothers christened themselves Peke, later revising it to Peck. The passenger manifest listed their occupation as farmers.

Although brother Michael elected to stay in Halifax, young Martin travelled north to Fort Cumberland, where he met Maria Sophia Kuntz, a fellow German émigré five years his junior. The couple married in 1760 and ten children soon followed — seven boys and three girls.[3] Martin was a yeoman, surviving through subsistence farming on rented parcels of land. Land was the surest, and often only, route to wealth in the colonies, and Martin Peck astutely surmised that without it, he was doomed to a life of penury. The only means of securing his share was the Crown land lottery. Like countless other applicants, Peck could do nothing more than cast his lot and wait.

In 1786 Martin Peck was granted five hundred acres in Cumberland Township, but the offer came too late.[4] Hoping for better luck in the recently created province of New Brunswick, the family had relocated north to the tiny parish of Hillsborough. Though tempted to return to Cumberland, Peck opted to sell off his acreage, wagering his family's future on New Brunswick's untapped possibilities.[5] Fortune smiled again in 1789, when Martin was awarded another parcel of land — a fertile tract of 237 acres — this time in Hillsborough.[6] Toiling shoulder to shoulder with a small band of recent German immigrants, the Pecks began to cultivate their modest homestead.

Despite their shared heritage, Martin's caustic nature led to a few minor skirmishes with his new neighbours. Twice he was sued over trivial matters. In each instance, judgments were entered against him when he failed to appear at trial, and he was ordered to pay small settlements to the plaintiffs.[7] Otherwise, the Peck family was unremarkable, hard-working if somewhat impoverished, and destined to leave little mark on history.

Given such modest roots, it is hardly surprising that no narrative survives of Jacob's childhood years. There are no diaries, letters, or family artifacts in the public or private archives. No direct evidence remains of the myriad childhood traumas that undoubtedly contributed to Jacob's questionable character — his lack of empathy, his rampant dishonesty, his need to control others. If he suffered abuse, neglect, or abandonment, it seems to have affected only young Jacob; there are no indications that older brother Martin Jr. or younger brother Leonard shared Jacob's grandiose delusions or dark personality traits. Although neither achieved great financial or professional success, Jacob's brothers, by all accounts, were decent, upstanding citizens. Certainly, neither resorted to criminal endeavours or had any significant run-ins with the law.

Aside from a brief note announcing his birth, the first mention of Jacob Peck in the historical record occurs in 1770, when at age five he was counted in the Nova Scotia census. By 1783, he was "a young man without family, no account of stock or grain,"[8] as noted in a registry of Hillsborough, although in fairness to Peck, he was only eighteen years old.

Jacob shared his father's conviction that land was the gateway to riches. In 1791 Jacob and his brother Martin Jr. each tried their hand in the land lottery but were denied.[9] Jacob's petition for the grant, however, is informative of its own accord. First, it contains one of Jacob Peck's earliest documented deceptions. In it, he described himself as a young man "about Twenty years of age,"[10] despite being just shy of his twenty-seventh birthday. Perhaps he believed the government looked favourably on requests from younger men. Second, the petition is a master class in grandiloquent fawning. In an era renowned for formal and flowery rhetoric, Peck's petition was particularly obsequious, even cloying, in its language and tone. It smacked of overreaching, and possessed an almost childlike notion of how the educated gentry expressed themselves. The petition offers a fascinating glimpse into Peck's already twisting psyche.

At the turn of the nineteenth century, the nascent province of New Brunswick — only recently seceded from neighbouring Nova Scotia — structured its local government into counties, each further subdivided into parishes. Despite the name, parishes had nothing to do with organized religion; in point of fact, at the time, most parishes lacked churches. Each parish administered its day-to-day affairs through the annual appointment of parish officers, who had limited scope to oversee their charges.[11] Posts included a diverse and bewildering array of purviews, including Surveyor of Fishes, Examiner of Butter, Hog Reeve, and Sealer of Leathers. Certain posts conferred far greater status on their holders than did more questionable appointments — Surveyor of Highways was infinitely preferable to Inspector of Thistles. Instead of formal elections, appointments were made by the gentlemen of the county's annually empanelled grand jury, who selected officers from the county's landholders and freemen. That said, it was not uncommon for the socially ambitious to lobby for loftier appointments.

Parish officers received little or no compensation for their labours. Depending on the position, certain appointees collected taxes or fees, some (or all) of which ended up in their own pockets. The vast majority, however, garnered no salary. Indeed, the post could just as readily cost its occupant money, should an officer abuse his station. The same legislative act that created the posts also stipulated a fine for "being guilty of any neglect or misbehaviour."[12] The penalty was stiff: forty shillings for each offence.

Despite their humble roots, the Peck brothers held their fair share of parish offices.[13] Martin Jr., four years Jacob's senior, was first appointed as constable for Hillsborough in 1790, a relatively low-level post with little real authority. Two years later, Jacob joined his brother in the ranks as constable. Although Jacob held the post for only a year, Martin retained the title for most of the decade, a clear indication of each man's perceived suitability to the job. Through excessive striving, rather than an excess of work ethic, Jacob managed to climb the social ladder ever so slightly when he was named Surveyor of Highways in 1799, a post he also lost after only one term. As with all aspects of his life, Peck's supposedly selfless public service was a ruse designed to disguise his true intent. Simultaneously obsessed with his own social rank while flagrantly disregarding the status and authority of others, Jacob Peck was a fundamentally envious man, desperate to inspire envy in others in a world that paid him little heed.

As the century turned, Jacob — then thirty-five — finally left the family home and set out on his own. In 1800 he moved north and west, to the parish of Salisbury. There, he rented a small plot of land and began farming. The next year, unaware of his past shortcomings, the grand jury of Salisbury voted to make Jacob Peck a constable. In 1803 he wormed his way up the hierarchy when he was named Fence-viewer, although many would dismiss it as a lateral move. In 1804 he was back to serving as Surveyor of Highways. That no appointment lasted beyond one term suggests he again failed to distinguish himself in any of his allotted roles. Still, for Jacob Peck, no opportunity for self-aggrandizement went unseized.

If Peck's social status was unremarkable, his place in the community's religious hierarchy was downright suspect. There is no evidence he ever set foot in a church or meeting house, much less a schoolhouse. What, if any, religious training Jacob Peck acquired prior to setting out on the itinerant circuit escapes all recorded history. How and when he was exposed to the New Light movement is equally nebulous. All that can be said with any certainty is that Jacob was raised Protestant, like his father before him. Equally certain is that Peck — devoid of empathy, humility, and simple common sense — was in no position to instruct others how to live a righteous life.

Unable to rise in the parish's political ranks, Peck saw preaching as a fast track to respect and social acceptance. Peck's desperate gambits for upward mobility meant he would never be satisfied as a run-of-the-mill catechist, street-corner missionary, or colporteur content to foist Bibles on those willing to take them. His undisguised quest for deference demanded more.

The widely reported notion that Peck was a Baptist was born in Reynolds's 1898 article, which referred to him as "another revivalist" in the Baptist tradition espoused by renowned preacher Joseph Crandall and others.[14] In his 1984 study, David Graham Bell notes the lack of discernible Baptist teachings in any of Peck's sermons. Indeed, there was little religious content of any stripe in Peck's revivals. His "lurid declamations" focused on a Doomsday message, warning of the fast-approaching End of Days.[15] His "sermons," those periodic feints of piety that bracketed his revivals, were otherwise devoid of religious imagery or doctrine. Peck's knowledge of Scripture appears limited to popular children's homiletics, including the Nativity and the parable of John the Baptist. As for Reynolds's painting Peck as a Baptist, it seems a case of mistaken identity by association. A number of prominent Baptist ministers, including Joseph Crandall and Henry Steeves, were among Peck's Salisbury neighbours.[16] As with all would-be socialites prone to name dropping, Peck undoubtedly used these acquaintances to buy his entry into a new community. As for his preaching style, Peck's embrace of the hellfire revival format had more to do with his inherent vanity and theatricality than with any specific religious doctrine. The peripatetic pastor cared little for advancing the glory of God; the only deity Peck served was Peck.

Additional insight into Jacob's character comes from his treatment of the women in his life. The 1803 census records Jacob Peck as living in Salisbury with a woman and two children. The identity of the woman remains a mystery, as does Peck's relationship to the children. Although they were, in all probability, his progeny, it is possible he had taken up with a widow and her children. What is certain is that their union was not sanctioned by any church or civil authority, nor were the children ever formally acknowledged as Peck's offspring.

Within a year, Jacob clearly had had a change of heart: in the winter of 1804, he became engaged to Joyce Alrod.[17] Joyce could not have been Peck's woman in Salisbury, as she was a resident of New Canaan, west of Salisbury, at the time of their betrothal. What became of Peck's Salisbury paramour and the children is lost to history.

Peck's romance with Joyce Alrod was not fated to last. Within weeks of securing the marriage bond, Peck travelled the circuit to Shediac Parish and there his life changed dramatically. The marriage to Alrod never took place. It would be comforting to believe Joyce changed her mind following Peck's legal difficulties, but given the times and the nature of the bridegroom, it is far more likely that Peck broke their engagement.

If Peck was at all broken-hearted, he did not weep for long. On Christmas Eve, 1806, Jacob Peck married Ann Horsman of Moncton Parish.[18] This time, the marriage was legitimate. The ceremony followed the publication of banns and was certified by William Sinton, Esquire — Justice of the Peace and Quorum for Salisbury Parish. The Horsmans were a prominent Moncton family and it was clearly a case of Jacob "marrying up."

Ann Horsman Peck left little trace in the public archives. History records no particulars of her appearance or her upbringing. The union of Jacob Peck and Ann Horsman produced no children. There are no clear indications of how long the marriage lasted or how happy it was. There is no record of what became of Ann. The location, cause, and time of her death were not marked for posterity. Although of higher social rank, Ann ultimately lacked Jacob's notoriety and capacity for mayhem. She was afforded little more than a footnote in history, doomed by her poor choice of husband.

Jacob Peck's rather cavalier attitude toward women provides one last vital clue as to his true nature, one it seems he went to great lengths to hide. Peck's brief dalliance with Joyce Alrod is preserved for the ages in a single document: a marriage bond secured on December 10, 1804. As a newcomer to Salisbury Parish with no established ties, Peck was obliged to obtain a marriage bond, the precursor to a marriage licence. It was a bond in the literal sense — Peck had to present the not inconsiderable "sum of Five Hundred Pounds current Money of the said Province" to have leave to marry.[19] Despite all efforts to the contrary, Peck remained a poor yeoman with no family money. To secure the permit, he sought out the services of a bondsman. Ichemial "Neke" Ayers was a part-time bondsman and full-time tavern owner in nearby Sackville.[20] For the right price, Neke agreed to post the bond on Jacob's behalf. Both men had to be present when the bond was secured. The actual document was a form completed by the county clerk and signed by both Peck and Ayers. On December 10, the clerk entered the relevant information in the spaces allotted in a distinctive, if not terribly legible, hand. He then handed the form to each man to sign. Neke Ayers affixed his signature in a clear, bold hand. The document was then passed to Jacob Peck.

Peck's affirmation on that bond heads this chapter. As was the practice of the day when dealing with an illiterate signatory, the clerk wrote out Peck's name, in the same distinct hand as the remainder of the document. Peck then made his mark, an X representing his signature.

Only three surviving signatures are attributable to Jacob Peck.[21] The earliest, which tops Chapter One, is from Peck's 1791 land grant petition, a document he did not sign in public. The marriage bond is the second, and it is the only instrument Peck was forced to sign in the presence of others. The final signature appends Peck's 1810 land grant petition, another privately signed document, and bears a striking resemblance to that of his younger brother, Leonard, whose autograph follows Jacob's on the petition.

The preacher's 1804 marriage bond — an unnecessary and expensive licence for a union that was never consummated — inadvertently reveals his closely guarded secret: for all his feigned education and purported Bible study, Jacob Peck was illiterate.

The Mark

Amos Babcock [1]

Amos Babcock was an entirely uncomplicated man. He possessed neither
a complex mind nor a tortured emotional landscape. He knew well his
limitations and his strengths. He lacked education but was strong of back
and limb. Although he was not afraid of hard work, his indecisiveness
had cost him more than one job. Easily intimidated and highly reverential
to those in authority, he constantly feared others knew more than he. But
Amos knew one thing for certain: he knew of God's power and might.
Whatever his own mortal failings, Amos trusted in the Lord to provide.
He needed only to prove himself worthy of God's grace and blessing.
Throughout his life, Amos sought refuge in the safe confines of the Bible,
eschewing the harsh realities of his lot. Having all but failed in this world,
Amos's only hope of salvation lay in the next.

Amos Babcock was born mid-century in Nova Scotia, although the
exact time or place eluded all forms of social tracking.[2] He was not
christened Amasa, the Acadian derivation of his name, as was widely but
erroneously reported. He was simply Amos.[3] He was the eldest child of
Jonathon Babcock Sr. and his wife, Lydia Larkin. The family soon grew
to include brothers Jonathon, Frederick, and George and sister Mercy.
Little is known of Amos's childhood beyond that it was spent along the
Nova Scotia shore of the Minas Basin.

The Babcocks were farmers without land, a precarious state of affairs akin to indentured servitude. After years of sharecropping, on July 21, 1761, Jonathon Sr. received a Crown land grant, a small allotment on the Pisquid River. In 1764 he traded the land for another parcel of more arable soil on the Kennetcook River. There the family maintained a small subsistence farm. Amos received little schooling, and in his second decade of life he set out to make his mark on the world.

At first, Amos wandered without aim or direction. While labouring in the seaside town of Kingsport, he met Dorcas Bennett, the daughter of Anna and Caleb Bennett. Dorcas — born on February 16, 1768, in the town of Horton, Nova Scotia — had just turned twenty. She was not a great beauty, but she was hardy and obedient. Neither Amos nor Dorcas had other prospects. The courtship was brief, highly supervised, and decidedly lacking in passion. Fortunately, a shared work ethic and strong religious convictions proved sufficient, and Amos and Dorcas were married at the Congressional Church in Chipmans Corner in 1788. The couple settled briefly in Cornwallis Parish, where their first child — a daughter they also named Dorcas — was born in 1790.

A promise of work lured the family across the Minas Basin to Hopewell Cape, New Brunswick, in 1791. The family continued to grow, welcoming sons Henry (1791) and Caleb (1794) and daughters Anne (1797), Mary (1798), Delilah (1800), and Sarah (1801). At the turn of the century, work again grew scarce for Amos.

Amos's brother Jonathon had also recently moved to New Brunswick, settling farther to the north. In 1798 Jonathon applied for a land grant in Westmorland County, but his petition was rejected.[4] Hoping to better his chances by taking up residence in the county, Jonathon, his wife Mary, and their children moved to Shediac Parish. The family crowded into a tiny house on the road to Cocagne, three miles from where the church of St. Martin's-in-the-Woods now stands. Jonathon worked a modest plot of land, trapping and hunting, and was slowly making a name for himself among his English-speaking neighbours. Jonathon's temperate success prompted Amos to consider relocating to the same area.

In the spring of 1803, Amos and Jonathon along with nine other applicants, including three of Jonathon's sons, petitioned the county for land.[5] Again, the petition was denied, but Amos remained optimistic that a future petition would prevail. Spurred by visions of free and bountiful land, Amos decided to move to Shediac. As the winter snows finally gave way to spring, Amos, Dorcas, and their children made their way north, joining a wave of other English-speaking settlers, including Samuel Cornwall and John Atkinson. This sudden influx of families into a land still dominated by wilderness resulted in a severe housing shortage. Adding to their woes, Dorcas had since given birth to two more daughters, Elizabeth and Amy. Amos and his ten dependents were forced to share Jonathon's congested house, a situation all agreed was far from ideal.

The Babcocks soon earned a reputation as "hard-working men, of little education, and of the type easily moved to go to extremes on occasions of excitement."[6] Amos's saving grace was his ardent religious faith. Unfortunately, Shediac had no church and no pastor. On Sunday evenings, Amos's family attended services at the home of William Hanington, who read from the Church of England's Book of Common Prayer.

William Hanington was something of a legend in the district, an errant bon vivant whose heart often ruled his head. He had sailed to the New World from his native London in the spring of 1785 after exchanging his property in England for five hundred acres in Shediac. Upon his arrival, he found his land inhabited by French squatters. He promptly evicted the Acadians and moved into their cabin. Although a few small bands of English-speaking settlers were living farther inland, Hanington was isolated in a community made up entirely of Acadian, Mi'kmaq, and Passamaquoddy members. The gregarious pioneer soon found himself lonely. Having forsaken the hurly-burly of London, the barren wilds of Shediac now stretched before William, full of the promise of adventure but devoid of suitable companionship.[7]

In 1792 he hired two Aboriginal guides and set out for Prince Edward Island, ostensibly in search of a wife. He and his Mi'kmaq escorts made the harrowing journey by canoe, opting for more stalwart modes of transport for his expeditions inland. According to local lore, Hanington was travelling by ox cart near Saint Eleanors when he saw a "comely young woman"[8] feeding the poultry in her father's barnyard.[8] The father was

Benjamin Darby, a Loyalist who lived to the ripe old age of one hundred, no small feat at the time. "It was a desperate case of first-sight affection,"[9] Hanington later said. He proposed on the spot, and to his shock and delight, his offer was gleefully accepted. Inquiring gently, he discovered the woman's name was Mary. There was no preacher on hand, so the ceremony was conducted by a local justice of the peace.

Later that same day, Mary and William returned to Shediac. No fewer than thirteen children followed, and the family quickly outgrew the squatters' cabin. In 1804, to accommodate his expanding brood, Hanington built the first frame house in the region, a sumptuous sprawling affair that towered high above his neighbours. It was in this imposing dwelling that religious services were held each Sunday.

Hanington, by then a prosperous trapper and merchant, was impressed by Amos Babcock's dogged work ethic and unassailable religious devotion. The town elder was also sympathetic to Amos's housing predicament. William first offered Babcock the one-room cabin he had vacated on the road to Cocagne. It had the benefit of being close to Jonathon's house but proved far too small for Babcock's sizable family. Generous to a fault, Hanington then proposed an alternative: there was a small house on the same road, recently vacated by a man named Peter Casey. Casey had sold the property on to John Atkinson, who was looking for a new tenant. Hanington agreed to lease the house on Babcock's behalf.[10]

Amos was touched by Hanington's largess but he was a proud man, unwilling to accept charity. Still, the cramped confines of his brother's home left him little choice. Unable to pay rent, Amos offered to provide Hanington with a steady supply of gaspereaux, a locally plentiful fish Amos often caught to feed his own family. Hanington happily shook hands on the deal, and without a moment's delay, Amos Babcock moved his family into their modest new home.

Collateral

Concerning the victim, Mercy Hall, little is now known.
— David Graham Bell, 1984[1]

It is a telling reflection of the era that the one woman central to this tale — the victim, Mercy Hall — warranted so little attention in both her sad life and her violent death. From the earliest renderings of the story, she is portrayed as little more than a catalyst for the actions of others, a casualty of her husband's cruelty, her brother's brutality, and a judicial system that disparaged her to garner a conviction.

Like her brother Amos, Mercy's origins also fell victim to the vagaries of time. All that can be confirmed is that she was younger than Amos and Jonathon and was born somewhere along the north shore of Nova Scotia. More is known about her later years, which is to say more is known about her husband.

In her late teens, Mercy Babcock — earnest, humourless, and plain — somehow caught the eye of Abner Hall Jr., whose life story is preserved for posterity. Abner was born on July, 4, 1749, decades before that date held any patriotic meaning, in a family that hailed from the fashionable village of Mansfield, Connecticut. He was the favoured son of his namesake, Abner Hall Sr., a man of relatively modest means, and his wife, Mary Ross. When Abner was in his teens, the family emigrated north to Canning, Nova Scotia, and it was there that he first set eyes on Mercy. Following a cursory courtship, the couple married on December 7, 1772, at St. John's Anglican Church in Canard, Nova Scotia. The pair then settled in nearby Cornwallis Parish, in the heart of the Annapolis Valley. Not willing to risk his future on the whims of the Crown land lottery, Abner borrowed a small stake from his father. On November 18, 1782, he purchased 182 acres of land in Annapolis County from a recent grant recipient, Alexander Brewster.[2] After clearing a small section of the acreage, Abner built a simple log cabin and began farming.

The marriage of Abner and Mercy was a loveless union, yet one that produced eight children. In the rural outposts of the Maritimes, the test of a man's mettle was his productivity, but a woman's worth was measured by her fecundity. On this count, Mercy proved her merit. The first child, a son named Samuel, arrived on March 6, 1774. Another six followed in quick succession: Lydia (1775), James (1776), Nathan (1779), John (1781), Elizabeth (1783), and Mary (1785).[3] It was with the birth of her final child — a son they called William, born on July 26, 1787 — that Mercy's fragile world began to unravel.

William's birth struck Mercy with a fever that left her mentally challenged, at least in Abner's lay opinion. Despite her best efforts, Mercy could no longer right herself. She took to her bed for days on end, failing to care for herself, her husband, or the children. Abner soon tired of his wife's moodiness and lethargy. At his wit's end, he banished Mercy from the house, casting her into the street with nothing more than the clothes on her back. Within weeks, he had replaced her with another, less morose woman who assumed the role of wife and mother with far greater vigour.

Homeless and with no viable means of support, Mercy turned to her brother Amos, begging him to take her in. Having recently secured the home from Hanington, Amos reluctantly agreed. Rumour has it he did not discuss the matter with Dorcas beforehand, an oversight that became a source of considerable, if unspoken, resentment in the marital bed.

And so, in the early days of 1805, Mercy Babcock Hall found herself in Shediac Parish, dependent on the goodwill of a timorous Amos and a disapproving Dorcas. Once ensconced, Mercy grew increasingly insular. She cut herself off from all but the immediate family and kept her interactions with them to a bare minimum. Judging from her behaviour, Mercy was likely depressed. In fact, the onset of her symptoms suggests postpartum depression, but such a clinical diagnosis exceeded the thinking of the day. Her brother simply believed she was sad — a sweet, sensitive soul for whom life proved too much to bear. Dorcas thought only that Mercy was weak. There was too much work to be done and Dorcas, every inch as pragmatic as Abner, had little patience for Mercy's moodiness. Dorcas Babcock, harried by the demands of nine children, led a far less introspective life. She bore the burden of Mercy without grace but also without vocal complaint. Dorcas soon found other ways to make her displeasure known.

On a typical evening in the claustrophobic confines of the Babcock home, nestled in a field off the road to Cocagne, just outside Shediac Cape, a ritual of sorts took place. After Dorcas had laid out the family's simple meal, husband and wife would stand at opposite ends of the long wooden bench that served as the family table. Amos would then call the children down from the loft, and those old enough would gather alongside, heads bowed at the ready. As their supper cooled on the table, Amos would lead his family in evening prayer. Mercy reportedly would stand on the periphery, welcome to join in the invocation but not in the family circle. Perhaps she took a moment to recite grace to herself; she had not spoken aloud in weeks. As the words of thanks drew to a close and the family sat down to their silent, perfunctory meal, Mercy would take a bowl and cross to the hearth. Spooning a few potatoes from the pot, she would wrap her shawl about her shoulders and, as was her custom, retire outside in the cold night air to eat her meal in solitude.[4]

Although few had any kind words for Mercy Hall in life, she was positively vilified in death. The assassination of her character began with the trial of her killer. If the purpose of the court proceedings was to extract some measure of justice for Mercy, no one informed the chief prosecutor, Ward Chipman. In the absence of a concrete motive for the slaying, Chipman elected to portray Mercy as a "reprobate,"[5] blaming the victim for being a burden on her brother. Chipman then took Mercy's posthumous lynching a step further, alluding to some prior grudge between Amos and his sister, as if that might justify her murder.

In later historical accounts of the crime, Mercy continued to be simultaneously overlooked and demonized. An 1805 newspaper account of the trial said simply that her death was "ignominious."[6] Reynolds's notorious 1898 account cast little light on Mercy, stating merely that she was of "melancholy disposition," "not allowed to eat with the others of the family."[7] These pitiful epitaphs became Mercy's sole defining characteristics, echoing through all subsequent accounts to the letter, save for Grant's 1983 reworking of the legend, in which he callously refers to Mercy as not "quite right in the head."[8] Mercy was dismissed as melancholic at a time when the label encompassed a wide spectrum of dark emotional afflictions and mental disturbances, with no hope of medical relief and no social support, save for religion.

As with all other aspects of her life, Mercy's religious beliefs were not fodder for the historical record. Court documents indicate she was present for at least one of Jacob Peck's sermons (the one held in Amos's house, where she lived), although nowhere was it stated that she participated in the revival. It is only in the popular accounts of the crime, written more than a century later, that whispers of Mercy's devotional practices appear, largely as a plot device to heighten the drama. Whether Mercy joined her siblings and attended Peck's revivals or even what her religious beliefs were remain matters of speculation. Perhaps it was Mercy's refusal to partake in Peck's hellfire sermons that led the petulant preacher to distrust or even to despise her. Why Peck ultimately targeted her remains a mystery. That Peck targeted her was undeniable, as the evidence will soon reveal.

Best Laid Plans

[signature: Wm. Hanington][1]

The first residents of Shediac Parish were not drawn to the area because of its picturesque landscape, although the coastline does possess a certain rugged beauty. They came because the land was free. To encourage settlement in the desolate province, as well as to bolster the king's sovereign claim to the land, the Crown granted great swatches of territory to those willing to occupy and work it. That is, if the willing parties were of the right sort. For one man, however, the lure of the northeastern shore was not gratis real estate but a true *cri du cœur*, a call of the wild that sailed clear across the Atlantic and found its way into a fishmonger's shop in London.

That call echoed in the heart of William Hanington, a man destined to become Shediac's first English-speaking settler. Consumed with errant wanderlust and an overly romantic notion of the Americas, Hanington was exactly the sort of frontiersman the king was hoping to attract. Had Hanington owned a map, however, in all likelihood he would not have heeded the call.

Born in London in 1759, Hanington was the son of a prosperous fish merchant destined to follow in his father's footsteps. London's charms, however, were lost on young William, who became convinced his future lay in the untamed wilds of the New World.[2] In 1783, twenty-four years of age and still landlocked in England, William at last saw his chance to break free of his domineering father. After making a series of discreet inquiries among his friends and acquaintances, Hanington reached a rather unorthodox arrangement with a British army officer named Joseph Williams. Unbeknownst to the fishmonger, the two men agreed to swap land. William Hanington traded a highly valued London property — the lone asset to his name and a recent inheritance — for the five hundred acres Joseph Williams had been granted in Shediac.[3] The jury was out as to whether Hanington got the short end of the stick in the deal, although after hearing the news, his father never doubted his son had been taken for a rube. Adding insult to financial injury, Williams told Hanington the Shediac parcel was "adjoining the city of Halifax," a perfect location for young William, who planned to fish and run an import-export business.

In 1785, his father's condemnation still ringing in his ears, Hanington set sail for Halifax and his new life in the New World. As the ship docked in Nova Scotia, William Hanington discovered his father's warnings were not far wrong. He soon learned that the land was far from Halifax-adjacent, as Williams had claimed. It was, in fact, some 190 miles away, in what later would become an entirely different province, New Brunswick.

Undaunted by the setback and unwilling to concede his mistake, Hanington made the trek to Shediac on foot through treacherous snows, hiking over the Cobequid Mountains dragging a sled laden with his meagre worldly possessions. A glutton for punishment, Hanington later repeated the arduous journey to and from Halifax in the spring, travelling almost four hundred miles on horseback to buy a frying pan and other household necessities in the port city.

Driven to prove his father wrong and possessed of an almost inhuman work ethic, Hanington made the most of his geographic blunder. He began trapping beaver and trading furs with the local First Nations tribes. A quick study with an ear for languages, he soon became proficient in the lingua franca, although he was forced to learn their customs through trial and error. One nearly fatal error occurred in his first year of trading.

William had purchased a particularly fine beaver pelt from a young Mi'kmaq. That night, the tribal chiefs appeared at his home. They claimed the beaver had been hunted out of season, the penalty for which was death. Hanington, accurately assessing the situation, denied buying the pelt. The chiefs left, skeptical and clearly dissatisfied.

Hanington quickly ran into the forest and buried the skin. Minutes later, the chiefs returned with a war party, threatening to kill Hanington, his wife, and young son. Hanington again denied buying the pelt. Thinking on his feet, he reminded one chief they had eaten salt together, an important sign of friendship among the Mi'kmaq. The gambit bought William a few hours' grace, but for the next seven days, the war party returned every evening, demanding the beaver hide. They threatened him with knives and tomahawks but William never wavered. As the threats turned violent, Hanington and his wife grew terrified. Mary implored him to return the pelt but Hanington suspected that producing the skin at this point would mean death.

Luck and tradition fell in Hanington's favour. According to tribal law, the chiefs could not kill Hanington without first finding the pelt. By burying it, Hanington had saved his own skin. Eventually, the tribe grew weary of the nightly showdown and moved on. For his part, Hanington made a point of educating himself about the local edicts — he never repeated his novice mistake.

As the century turned, William Hanington continued to sharpen his business acumen. In 1803 he opened the first store in Shediac Parish. From a modest storefront, he traded his furs and sold lumber, hardware, and dry goods. Given the financial hardships of his clientele, payment was often delayed and sometimes taken in forms other than money. Locals maintained accounts and made good when they were able.[4]

Hanington's adventure in mercantile has a curious footnote in the death of Mercy Hall. Local gossip held that Amos Babcock purchased the knife he used to kill his sister from Hanington's store a few days before the murder. While such titillating whispers add a certain immediacy to the tale — and would have provided the crucial element of premeditation during the trial — no evidence of any such transaction is preserved in the historical record. No account books or receipts of Hanington's business survive in the public archives. Although his shop was the lone mercantile in Shediac at that time, descriptions of his merchandise indicate Hanington never sold clasp blades. Furthermore, a folding knife was so fundamental a part of the tool kit of a journeyman that Babcock likely had acquired such a necessity in his youth. ·

History has a funny way of miscasting key players. William Hanington might not have sold Amos Babcock the murder weapon, but he nevertheless would play a crucial role in the drama about to unfold.

act 2
Premeditation

scienter [Latin, "knowingly"] A degree of knowledge that makes a person legally responsible for the consequences of an act; a mental state consisting of an intent to deceive or manipulate.

Vicious Propensity

*The melancholy affair that has lately happened here
has induced me to trouble you with a description of the
proceedings of a Jacob Peck of Potquodiach previous to
that misfortune.... The people here met on Sundays and
Thursday evenings to worship God. I attended meetings
as long as they were conducted with propriety but the
unfortunate man Amos Babcock turned preacher and so
much confusion took place that I forbade any of my family
from attending — not withstanding, my wife did go two
or three times afterwards.*

— William Hanington, 1805[1]

William Hanington, still smarting from being bested in the land deal,
vowed never again to fall prey to a swindler. All evidence to the contrary,
he prided himself on being an excellent judge of character. It did not take
long for him to distrust Jacob Peck, despite the preacher's duplicitous
best efforts. Indeed, it would be fair to say that the unerringly polite
Hanington disliked the impolitic Peck from the start. Hanington was
not alone in his assessment of the damnable evangelist. Amos Babcock's
brother Jonathon shared many of Hanington's misgivings about Peck.
Fiercely protective of the life he had built and the village he called home,
William Hanington took it upon himself to monitor Peck's movements
within the parish. The town-elder-turned-amateur-sleuth had no way
of knowing, weeks later, how crucial his observations would be.

Jacob Peck blithely went about his business, wholly undeterred. As
was his practice, Peck began his ministry in Shediac by usurping the
existing services. He noted where and when religious gatherings were

held and who officiated. He ingratiated himself, making subtle inquiries of passing residents, asking where a newcomer might find the word of God. One passing resident — Amasa Killam — invited the town's newest arrival to his home to share in that night's informal services. Peck had been in Shediac less than twenty-four hours.

Arriving at the Killam homestead, Peck made himself known to the other English settlers gathered, meeting each in turn and eventually securing a blanket invitation to participate in any future religious services. Careful not to play his hand too early, Peck did not preach at the meeting; he was there merely to observe. By the end of the meeting, Peck had won the confidence of several community leaders, including Killam, John Welling, and Samuel Cornwall. Learning of their visitor's profession, Amasa Killam invited Peck to lead the service the following evening, January 8, a mere two days after Peck first set foot in the secluded enclave.

As fate would have it, the meeting was held in the newly acquired home of Amos Babcock. It was the first time Amos had welcomed neighbours to his house for religious devotions. With his customary humility, Babcock greeted the stranger and ceded the pulpit to his unexpected guest. Babcock then received his neighbours, struggling to make room for all within the cabin's timbered walls. News of a visiting pastor brought out the curious, and the crowd swelled to include the usual congregants — including William Hanington and his wife, Mary — as well as a few less frequent attendees. As she was a beholden guest in the house, Mercy was unquestionably present during the sermon, although we are left to speculate whether she actively participated.

Whatever the conservative supplicants were expecting, they were unprepared for what was unleashed. Jacob Peck announced his arrival with booming voice and exalted flourish. The effect was ineffable, shocking the stunned assemblage into cowering submission. As he paced and proselytized, Peck's message to the faithful was both delusional and oddly non-denominational. Peck declared he was not who he appeared to be — a parody of understatement. With the repetitious pleas of a drunkard, Peck murmured time and again that he was, in truth, John the Baptist, delivered unto them to save their immortal souls After a dozen iterations, it dawned on Hanington that the preacher's revelation was not intended as parable or metaphor but as an actual declaration of identity. Peck truly believed he had once baptized Jesus Christ.

Having established his false credentials, Peck segued into his teachings. His sermon was as bleak as it was chaotic. Without ceremony, Jacob decreed that the End of Days was at hand. In a dream, he had seen a worldwide apocalypse destined to destroy humanity. The End Times were near, but the good people of Shediac need not fear. As John the Baptist, the precursor of Christ Himself, Peck offered salvation and the promise of eternal life in paradise for all those who believed his words and accepted his leadership. A true all-or-nothing proposition, Peck's call to the faithful garnered no immediate takers.

Hanington, for one, was not readily swayed. Peck's apocalyptic vision was not born of a sailor's sense of imminent danger but a narcissistic need to place himself in the eye of every storm. From where Hanington sat, the entire farce was not about the worship of God but the self-promotion of a clearly unstable lunatic.

While William Hanington remained unmoved, the performance yielded mixed reviews from the other acolytes in attendance. To deliver his doomsday message, Peck had wholeheartedly embraced a theatricality never before seen by the rural yeomen assembled. Peck's bravado bore little affinity to the sombre, sedate services previously held in Shediac. His was a true hellfire-and-brimstone ministry, replete with chanting, singing, and dancing. Refusing to be denied, Peck beseeched them to cast off their societal constraints and release the true Holy Spirit within. He entreated his followers to enter into trances and speak in tongues. Prophesies, exclamations, and spontaneous healings were rewarded in an almost Pavlovian manner. As the night wore on, inhibitions were shed as some of the congregants embraced this new-found fervour. Others simply stood by, dumbfounded. It is possible a few remained out of curiosity, enjoying the spectacle purely for its entertainment value.[2]

In a night of strange and wondrous firsts, there was no end to the queer happenings Peck had in store. At one point, amid the babel that had colonized the room, "they were alarmed by a great noise, as if something of a great weight and force had fallen on the upper floor. Some of them thought the French were firing against the house."[3] The commotion frightened the assembly into a momentary silence. Peck, capitalizing on an unforeseen event, used the distraction to bring the crowd to heel. William Hanington used it to make a hasty exit. As he stepped outside, he was surprised to see light on the horizon, the dawn of January 9. He was later shocked to learn that those he had left behind, including his wife, Mary, continued praying and prostrating themselves for another twenty-four hours straight. Leading the charge was the evening's host, Amos Babcock.

Initially timid, Amos Babcock soon found himself swept up in the ecstasy, blossoming under the aegis of this most peculiar stranger. According to Hanington, "Jacob Peck supported Amos Babcock in everything he said or did."[4] Throughout the evening, Peck repeatedly singled out Babcock, lavishing him with excessive attention and praise. Although he never relinquished control, Jacob Peck manoeuvred Babcock into the spotlight, declaring his every utterance to be Divine gospel. Babcock began to assume the role of preacher under Peck's relentless tutelage, leading the congregation in boisterous prayer as they prepared for the coming Rapture. Overflowing with a chanting, sweaty, teaming mass in the throes of a celestial mania, the room and its occupants grew fetid and dank as the hours wore on.

Then — as mysteriously as it had begun — the revival abruptly ended. The world had not ended and their faith let them live to see another day, although Peck likely took the credit. As morning dawned on January 10, a full thirty-six hours after the sermon began, Jacob Peck collapsed in exhaustion. The laity, rousing themselves from a stupor induced by dehydration, lack of sleep, and hunger, quickly gathered their heavier clothing and made their way home in the austere light of daybreak. It was, without question, the most bizarre, exciting thing to happen in the parish since its inception.

Despite the seeming chaos, there was method in Peck's madness. For all the pandemonium, the key to Peck's unspoken strategy rested in his unwavering support of Amos Babcock's trances and prophesies. Guided

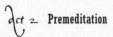 ct 2 **Premeditation**

by instincts he neither acknowledged nor understood, the preacher targeted Amos for special attention. Babcock was likely chosen because he appeared weak and gullible and was willing to accept Peck's delusions without challenge.

The arrangement was not without mutual benefit. Amos, unaccustomed to having his opinions taken seriously, was flattered by Peck's open admiration. Others — most notably William Hanington — dismissed Babcock's notions of God as pedantic and facile. His was a punishing, vengeful God in need of constant appeasement and silent sacrifice. Amos Babcock, long given to cowering in the face of a wrathful Lord, had at last found a harbour for his tempest-tossed fears and naive convictions. Peck had freed Babcock from such constraints, guiding him to a more intimate communion with his Saviour. Pity it was all a sham.

Playing soundly on Babcock's innate fears, Peck promised to prepare Amos for the coming Rapture. In Peck, Amos found a fellow deluded believer, someone who shared his fatalistic interpretation of the Bible. If Peck spoke the Lord's true word — and it was obvious to all Amos believed that he did — the End Times were at hand, a nihilistic notion Babcock found oddly comforting. Amos's earthly struggles finally could cease. Freed from the burdens of the temporal world, he need only focus his remaining energies on the coming glories of heaven.

Though guised as religious dogma, Jacob Peck's grooming of Amos Babcock was far more secular in nature. What Peck sought was not the salvation of Amos's soul, nor that of any other in attendance. His goal was neither deliverance nor redemption. Peck's aim was simple: complete control of Babcock's mind, body, spirit, and will.

What motivated Peck was not money, for Babcock had none. Nor was it power, as Amos held no office or title. Peck craved obedience, subservience, and admiration. He sought unconditional devotion and immutable respect. He was looking for a follower in the truest sense of the word. He found all of this and more in the guileless figure of Amos Babcock.

That Peck had done nothing to deserve such allegiance was precisely the point. It was Amos's unquestioning, unsophisticated soul that Peck wanted. Those blessed with more suspicious natures were immune to

Peck's shallow charms. It was Babcock's inherent insecurity, decency, and naïveté that left him so vulnerable to Peck's manipulations.

For all its theatrics, the madhouse revival proved little more than a smokescreen, a clamorous lure designed to entice an unsuspecting tyro. In the midst of the Second Great Awakening, cloaked in a mantle of religious fervour and spiritual devotion, the seduction of Amos Babcock had begun.

Act 2 Premeditation

Neglect and Regret

In the pantheon of criminals and miscreants, few possess a less auspicious genesis than Amos Babcock. His ignoble life of crime began with the neglect of some livestock under his care. As criminal acts go, the offence was relatively benign, but it was the first unmistakable warning sign, a harbinger of things to come. All agreed it was entirely out of character for the otherwise gentle-hearted man.

The red flag was raised in late January. Peck's demented revivals had continued unabated since his arrival. Only the location and congregants changed. No one seemed to notice that the End Times, long promised, had yet to materialize. Despite Peck's jeremiads of doom, Amos remained a devoted follower. The lone drawback was that the days-long meetings left him drained and lethargic in the face of his Herculean work schedule. Compounding his worries, Amos's once-plentiful stockpile of gaspereaux had been completely exhausted. In addition to his wife and nine children, Babcock now had another mouth to feed: his sister Mercy, although in truth she ate very little. The homeless, penniless preacher, Jacob Peck, had also become a permanent guest at the Babcock table, a form of tithe Peck considered his due. As a consequence, Babcock fell short on his promise of fish in lieu of rent to William Hanington.

Initially, Hanington was sympathetic to Babcock's plight, and once again proposed an alternative arrangement. Through good fortune and foresight, Hanington had amassed considerable holdings of livestock, including several head of young cattle. Hanington suggested Babcock overwinter the herd, providing for their shelter and feed during the harshest months, to clear his debt. Babcock readily agreed to the scheme and had personally supervised the transfer of the cattle to the barn adjacent to his home in the last days of January. With the herd firmly ensconced, Amos began caring for them with a diligence Hanington found almost touching. The town elder was pleased with the arrangement, confident his valuable stock was in competent hands.

During the second week of February, while conducting business in the town, Hanington was approached by Joseph Poirier, a French settler whose property lay to the west of the fields near Amos Babcock's house. After the pair exchanged their customary warm greetings, Poirier relayed some troubling news. Over the course of the previous week, Poirier had had occasion to pass the paddock housing Hanington's herd and had been shocked by the shameful condition of the cattle that appeared malnourished, sickly, and in danger of succumbing to the elements. Scarcely believing his ears, Hanington hurried to the paddock and saw first-hand the sad state of his herd. The animals huddled listless and weakened, with no food or water in sight. Enraged, William Hanington stormed from the paddock to have a few harsh words with his wayward tenant.[1]

The journey home did little to lessen his fury. That afternoon — February 12, 1805 — Hanington summoned Babcock to his home, intent on calling the man to account. Within the hour, Babcock arrived, hat in hand. In due course and heated tone, Hanington described his encounter with Joseph Poirier, as well as his own observations. Babcock offered no excuse or explanation. When asked why the animals had no feed, Amos simply replied, "the Lord will provide."[2] Babcock, adamant the Rapture was at hand, no longer felt the need to worry about earthly matters. He had put his faith fully, blindly, utterly in God and, by extension, Jacob Peck.

Faced with such fancy, Hanington fought to keep his ire at bay. He considered himself a religious man, but he was first and foremost a businessman. As a fellow man of God, he wanted to respect Babcock's convictions, even if he could not bring himself to accept the man's preposterous beliefs.

Act 2 **Premeditation**

But Hanington was equally disgusted by Peck's poisonous hold on the community. Since the preacher's arrival, Hanington had watched as curiosity had given way to obsession among his followers. What began as a lark — just another in a long line of itinerant ministers who had descended upon the town — had now turned into a pestilence ravening through the village, leaving madness and chaos in its wake.

Seated at his handsomely carved desk in his elegantly appointed den, Hanington was master of his domain, an unassailable (if still unofficial) ruler of the parish.[3] Yet he was overcome with a world weariness he could no longer disguise. In the few scant weeks since Peck first set foot in Shediac, the mongrel cleric had exhausted Hanington's normally boundless reserves of good humour and tolerance. The matter could not stand. At that moment, Hanington resolved to end the *malis avibus* consuming the district. He would set Peck to right, sending him packing if necessary. But first, there was the far more pressing matter of Amos Babcock.

Turning back to his recalcitrant tenant, a man Hanington had grown to trust and consider a friend, the de facto ruler of Shediac made his decision known. He told Amos in no uncertain terms he would remove the cattle immediately if conditions did not improve. Eviction was also not out of the question if the situation was not soon sorted. With that the meeting ended. Exhausted, Hanington elected to leave the issue of Peck for another day, when his strength and patience had returned in full measure.

The apologue of the abandoned herd forewarned of Amos's deteriorating mental state. He had already begun to shirk his earthly duties, retreating deeper into a fantasy world in which the Lord alone assumed responsibility for every conceivable want and need. The timing of the confrontation is also a critical benchmark in establishing the rate of Babcock's descent into madness. Over the next twenty-four hours, Amos Babcock's crime spree would escalate from animal cruelty to fratricide.

The Messenger

Mary Hanington[1]

On the western shore of Shediac Harbour lies the Cape, a particularly fine stretch of land that has been hearth and home to some of the most prominent families in Westmorland County. Today, it is the site of Younglands,[2] a grand estate built in 1927 by J.W.Y. Smith, a provincial politician of some distinction and grandson of Sir Albert Jones Smith, a controversial Member of Parliament for Westmorland and a famous opponent of Confederation. Younglands is now owned by a Catholic order, but not far from its stately grounds there once stood another home, a tad less ostentatious perhaps but still splendid in its heyday.

In 1804 William Hanington erected the first wooden frame house in Shediac Parish, on the wharf road in what is now Shediac Cape. While his neighbours made do in cabins cobbled together from "unbarked logs,"[3] Hanington built a showplace befitting his growing reputation as a merchant. Better still, it was capable of housing his enormous and ever-expanding family. While no trace of the house survives, it was crafted of hand-hewn boards and beams, and unlike the humble shacks of his fellows, it featured real walls rendered in split board and lathe, finished with a lime of burnt oyster shells. Despite its considerable charms, the house retained many less refined touches. Nails were still hand wrought and used sparingly. Water had to be bucketed from a nearby well, and the bake oven in the kitchen was a far cry from the modern cast-iron appliances cropping up in the grander estates to the south. The lone source of light was tallow candles, affixed in brass candlesticks. Yet, for all its rustic concessions, the Hanington house eclipsed its contemporaries in grandeur and prestige.[4]

Hanington was understandably proud of his fine home. It was a landmark in the district, where the rare homestead and cultivated fields soon dissolved into wilderness. In addition to the informal church services they held on Sundays, William and Mary often hosted their neighbours for lavish dinners or other community events. The family maintained an open door policy. Everyone in Shediac Parish knew the Haningtons, knew where they lived, and knew to treat them accordingly.

So it was not entirely beyond the pale for a knock at the door to come just as February 12, 1805, gave way to the wee small hours of the 13th. William Hanington, startled from his sleep, lit a candle, dressed quickly, and thundered down the stairs. Such a rude awakening never heralded good news.

Hanington opened the door, revealing the breathless and somewhat reluctant figure of a neighbour who, for reasons known only to the homeowner, was never identified by name in the countless witness statements future events soon engendered.[5] The messenger begged William's indulgence and apologized profusely for calling at such an ungodly hour. He had been sent to fetch Hanington and bring him to the home of John Welling. When Hanington asked why, he was told that the preacher, Jacob Peck, wanted Hanington to witness and record the startling prophesies unfolding at a revival taking place at Welling's even as they spoke.

Hanington could scarcely believe his ears. He had been wrenched from his bed in the middle of the night to play secretary to that fool evangelist. Hanington informed the messenger he had no intention of going out into the cold dark night to write down the rantings of a pack of lunatics and heretics. Having effectively shot the messenger, Hanington slammed the door and stormed back to bed. Suitably chastised, the unnamed neighbour sheepishly retreated into the night.

Upstairs, Hanington found his wife and son William standing in their bedclothes. Hanington told them it was nothing and to go back to bed, precisely as he intended to do. Mary hastened the child back to his bed and then joined her husband in the master suite.

Mary Hanington was every bit her husband's equal, remarkable at a time when women were still considered chattel. A Darby daughter through and through, Mary refused to suffer fools, gladly or otherwise, and was not above taking her husband to task when the need arose. Having spent the evening listening to William bluster about Babcock, starving cattle, and how their idyllic village had been torn asunder by the feeble rantings of a charlatan preacher, she knew sleep was no longer an option. Years of marriage had taught Mary, an unsentimental pragmatist, how best to handle her husband's mercurial moods. She would let him vent, all the while manoeuvring him back into bed. As they settled under the covers, William raged as he told Mary what he had been asked to do. With uncharacteristic venom, Hanington dismissed Peck's revivals and prophesies, saying "it was all a delusion, they wanted mad houses, not meeting houses."[6]

As William's ire cooled and peace once again descended, Mary snuffed out the candle and gave thanks for a quick end to the night's turmoil.

The house had barely settled into sleep when another pounding at the door echoed through the halls. This time Hanington was undone. Indignant, he threw off the covers and hurled himself down the stairs. As he threw open the door, braying bloody murder, he found yet another unnamed emissary. Peck was nothing if not obstinate, made all the more reckless by an unwarranted sense of entitlement. The revivalists were not to be so easily denied.

Cautiously, the new envoy delivered the message. Hanington stood dumbfounded as he was informed he needed to come straight away, that these sinners have "something to say before they die and they want it written down."[7] Sensing he would have no peace until he complied, Hanington told the messenger to run ahead and tell Peck he would soon follow. Although the timing was far from ideal, Hanington knew the moment to confront the profligate pastor had arrived.

Mary, gifted with an unerring ability to anticipate her husband's moods and needs, was already well ahead of him. Hanington returned to his bedchamber to find his wife scurrying about the room, preparing his clothes for a hasty departure. Hanington dressed quickly, cursing Peck the entire time. Mary offered her only rebuke of the night, admonishing her husband to mind his language while gesturing to the wall. She knew full well their young son, William, was laying in his bed in the next room, soaking in every word. She was, of course, right. Years later, William Jr. recalled overhearing his father tell his mother, "perhaps I can convince them of their error"[8] — one of the less colourful suggestions offered up that night.

Pulling on his boots and a pair of snowshoes, Hanington bid his sensible wife farewell and headed out into the frigid night. The endless trek to the home of John Welling afforded him ample opportunity to hone his argument. As he stumbled through the heavy snow, the town's resident voice of reason was bellicose, ready to school Peck in the ways of civilized men. For her part, Mary relished the restored tranquility and offered up a silent prayer for both her husband and the pastor Jacob Peck. As much as she revered her husband, she remained undecided as to who would emerge victorious in their impending showdown.

act 3

Things done

inchoate offence A partially completed or imperfectly formed criminal act; a step toward the commission of a crime, the step in itself being serious enough to merit punishment; the three inchoate offences are attempt, conspiracy, and solicitation.

solicitation The criminal offence of urging, advising, commanding, or otherwise inciting another to commit a crime; a defendant is guilty of solicitation even if the command or urging was not directly communicated to the solicited person.

Hellfire

William Hanington and John Welling shared a unique bond: they had both married Darby girls. Benjamin Darby had raised his daughters to be strong willed, fiercely independent, and free spirited. William, of course, had his beloved Mary, the older sibling, while John had wedded her sister Elizabeth.

John Welling II was a British subject, transplanted to New York State and later driven north during the Loyalist exodus that succeeded the Revolutionary War. John and Elizabeth were living on Welling Point in what later became Prince Edward Island when they received an urgent letter from Mary Hanington.[2] She and William had taken up residence in Shediac Cape, surrounded by only a few other English-speaking compatriots. As garrulous as her husband, Mary was lonely and begged her sister to come live in New Brunswick to keep her company. After much debate, the Wellings agreed, heading across the Northumberland Strait in 1795.

The couple and their two sons — William and Frederick — moved into an abandoned log cabin near the Haningtons. Given his Loyalist background, John was favoured in the land lottery, quickly drawing a grant for 193 acres in what is now Shediac proper.[3] The couple set about building their new home, a far simpler affair than the sumptuous manor of their in-laws. It was at the door of that modest home that a very irate William Hanington found himself in the dead of night.

The frigid air had not softened Hanington's mood, nor had it prepared him for what he was about to witness. After exchanging a few cursory words with his brother-in-law, Hanington demanded to see Peck. He was led to one of the children's rooms. There he found more than a dozen people crowded into the small bedroom, rendering it claustrophobic and more than a little close. The smell alone revealed they had been there for some time.[4]

At the centre of the room were two teenage girls: Amos Babcock's oldest daughter, Dorcas, and Samuel Cornwall's eldest, Sarah. The girls lay supine on a crude wooden bed, arms extended over their heads, eyes fluttering half-closed. Their lips never stopped moving, even if no intelligible sounds escaped. At one point, the Babcock girl shouted that she "saw the French all going down to hell."[5] Turning to Hanington as if in a trance, her eyes vacant and black, she pleaded, "cannot you pray for their immortal souls?"[6]

Hanington's eyes at last landed on his nemesis, the preacher Jacob Peck, standing sentry over his odalisques on the bed, a malevolent shepherd with his vulnerable flock. His possession of them was literal and sickening. While stroking the girl's hair, he told Sarah Cornwall's father that his daughter "belongs to me and the Lord. She is an Angel of light."[7] The preacher, at last spying Hanington in the doorway, broke from the vile tableau, strode across the room, and grabbed hold of William's arm. He gestured broadly to his handmaidens on the bed and declared, "I am bound here; there is my epistle. There is John the Baptist."[8] According to Samuel Cornwall, Peck then screamed, "from them, I shall break and take my text."[9] Hanington wondered if they had all taken leave of their senses.

John Welling stepped forward, begging his brother-in-law's attention. He cleared a space on the bureau and placed there some paper, a pen and ink, and a candle. Welling then gestured to the makeshift desk. For what seemed an eternity, Hanington and Peck stood face to face, seething. Long simmering resentments and mistrust on both sides boiled over; the confrontation had begun. Peck said the girls had been wracked with visions all evening and demanded Hanington transcribe their prophesies verbatim. Turning to his followers, Peck swore it was to be a momentous occasion. He wanted every utterance, every note, preserved for posterity. William was loath to help the preacher, but decided he wanted the madness documented for his own reasons. Since it suited him to do so, Hanington began to capture the scene unfolding before him, struggling to put lunacy to paper.

He embarked on a survey of the room. He noted its occupants: Peck, John and Elizabeth Welling, the entranced girls astride the bed, fellow settlers Amasa Killam and Samuel Cornwall, and Lucy Bramble, a mere chit of a girl the same age as those laying transfixed at the centre of the storm. Hanington was saddened but not at all surprised to see Amos Babcock and his wife Dorcas were also in attendance.[10]

With Hanington in place, all eyes turned to Peck and his nubile acolytes. In the stark candlelight, the preacher became a striking caricature, etched with malice. After a moment of melodramatic silence, Jacob Peck turned a lecherous eye to the third girl in the room, Lucy Bramble. Pausing for effect, allowing time for the portent to gather, Peck's sonorous voice rang out. With casual indifference, Peck informed Lucy he "had seen her Sealed to Everlasting Destruction."[11] The cleric's prophesy stunned the girl and sent her reeling. Those assembled fell into frantic prayer. Amid the chanting, Sarah Cornwall suddenly drew silent, her eyes fluttering, her arms thrusting upward. She remained frozen, locked in that awkward stance for two or three minutes, eons for the huddled masses hungry for her next vision. Hanington thought the girl appeared to "not to be in her senses."[12] Despite her crazed countenance, it was all a facade, grand theatre for an undiscerning audience. What happened next revealed the true nature of Peck's ministry and the depths of his machinations. According to Hanington, "Jacob Peck would say 'she will prophecy this or that' & she hearing what he said, would fall into another trance & afterwards repeat nearly what he had said she would."[13]

To those not intoxicated by the preacher's stagecraft, it was clear the girls were nothing more than puppets parroting Peck's words. Having grown weary of Sarah Cornwall, the evangelist-cum-ventriloquist then turned his attentions to young Dorcas Babcock. Following the now-established pattern of give and take between Peck and his disciple, Dorcas began to forecast the coming Armageddon. It was Peck's favoured message, one he never tired of revisiting despite its chronic failure to become a reality. At Peck's urging, the girl cried that "this world would be drowned by a flood in a short time & that two people would be saved in an Ark."[14]

Once again, the proclamation shocked those assembled. Elizabeth Welling fervently prayed to God that the child's words were untrue. Whatever control Peck had over his teenage novice momentarily slipped. Hearing the hostess's plea, Dorcas tellingly replied that her words "did not come from God & that it hurt her Soul"[15] to say them — a statement that raises a troubling question about Dorcas Babcock's willing participation in the ordeal.

Unable to hold his tongue a moment longer, Amos Babcock pushed to the fore. He pleaded with his daughter, begging to know if God had shown her which two people were to be saved in the Ark. Without waiting for a prompt from Peck, Dorcas told her father that Mrs. Welling was to be saved. If Dorcas hoped to defuse the escalating tension, her gambit failed. Still faltering from Peck's vision of Lucy Bramble's eternal damnation, Elizabeth Welling asked Dorcas if "it was not Lucy she meant?"[16] The Babcock girl paused, pondering the question. Dorcas then revised her prophesy without consulting Peck, telling the anxious crowd that it was, in fact, Lucy who was destined to be saved.

Peck was nothing if not a consummate showman, able to read a crowd and respond to its ever-shifting mood. But Peck was a slave to two masters: his unquenchable need for attention and his malignant need to control. He once again took up the reins of the revival, bringing Dorcas back into the fold. After none too subtly telegraphing his message, the girl began to describe her latest prophesy. The dystopian vision remained the same, but perhaps sensing a change in the room, Peck now tempered it with some familiar biblical imagery and the faint hope of salvation.

Following the pastor's offstage directives, Dorcas again foretold of a world destroyed by flood. This time, it was man's great fortune that a

"Saviour would be born of a woman & laid in a manger in swaddling clothes."[17] The crèche reference served only to highlight Peck's facile knowledge of Scripture. That the Nativity and the Ark were the sole biblical allusions in Peck's repertoire is both telling and lamentable, reducing an entire theology to little more than slogans and mottoes. Peck's tenuous grasp of the Bible was a direct result of his inability to read it, a secret he kept well hidden from the faithful. Oblivious to their minister's limitations, the news of the coming Saviour momentarily cheered the revivalists.

Incensed by their joy, Peck's capricious nature reared its ugly head. No sooner had Dorcas forecast imminent salvation than Peck had her again declare the coming End of Days. This time, the world was to be consumed by a great fire, to which the crowd responded with an anticipated mix of terror and disbelief. To drive his point home, Peck told his followers directly: "it is likely the end of the world will be this night. The Angel of the Lord is gone out to seal the people."[18]

It was at this stage that Peck's message became pointed and personal. No longer content to predict a worldwide apocalypse, Peck now focused his dire predictions on his most devoted and gullible disciple, Amos Babcock. Peck had at his disposal a chilling and calculated weapon: Amos's own daughter. With reckless disregard for all consequences, Peck urged the girl to continue. Dorcas Babcock, long past the point of exhaustion and on the verge of tears, did as she was instructed.

Though broadcast to the masses, her final vision was intended solely for her immediate family. Dorcas lay silent and still, absorbing Peck's whispered dispatch. When at last the spell was broken, her words fell like daggers. With stilted tongue, as though struggling to speak in a language not her own, Dorcas professed that God had shown her the future. In her vision, her father Amos, mother Dorcas, and all her brothers and sisters would be saved, called to the Lord to live out their days at His right hand.[19]

Before Amos could rejoice, she continued. She screamed that her head ached, filled with horrific apparitions: seething lakes of fire, surrounded by writhing hordes of non-believers consumed in the flames of Hell. And in the midst of the final inferno stood her aunt, Mercy Hall. Peck's frantic mumbling persisted, with Dorcas's narration lagging seconds behind. Mercy was dead yet she did not burn. Casting a lone ray of light on Peck's stark vision, Dorcas saw Mercy as resplendent, with angelic wings of niveous feathers. In her mind's eye, Dorcas claimed to see Mercy as she came upon Amos and his children walking through the fields. Wrapping them in her glorious wings, Mercy cradled them to her bosom and carried them up to their Heavenly Father. Having safely spirited her brother and kin to the firmament, Mercy tumbled back to earth.

Dorcas collapsed on the bed. The vision was fully rendered. The prophesy was complete.

Peck's poisoned dart sank deep into the heart of its intended victim, the perfect double-edged foil. Amos was struck mute, awed by the Lord's vision of his future. God's message was clear: Judgment Day was truly at hand. It was to be that very night. Only one thing stood between Amos and salvation: Mercy must die that she might save him and his family. But for the death of his sister, it was the sign Amos had been waiting for, the message he so longed to hear. He would be Raptured. So great was his desperation to hear those words that he never stopped to question the authenticity of the message or its messenger. Wrapped in his comforting mantle of delusion and denial, Amos failed to recognize that the vision had come not from God or even from his own daughter. The prophet was Jacob Peck.

His message delivered, Jacob Peck no longer felt compelled to whisper or use the girls as his marionettes. He rose up and told the crowd he had a matter of great import to discuss. That very morning, he had personally received word from the king of England, conveyed to him by private letter from Saint John. The king revealed that a great reformation had taken place in England or France; the location was neither clear nor important. Peck raced ahead, stating that the king himself had prophesied there would be no more crowned heads left in Europe within ten years' time.[20] That the king's prophesy conflicted with Peck's own, in which the end of the world was imminent, escaped all notice or comment.[21] Faith is inherently blind. No one in attendance, including the skeptical Hanington, thought to challenge Peck or demand that he produce the letter as proof.

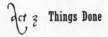 ct 3 **Things Done**

It was simply another entry in the endless parade of falsehoods, boasts, and mind games that were part and parcel of accepting Peck as God's interlocutor. [22]

With that one last, ludicrous conceit, Jacob Peck called a halt to the night's proceedings. He would never preach in Shediac Parish again.

Hanington finished his fraught scribbling, having captured every word. He now believed Peck was grotesque, dangerous, perhaps even insane. He wanted proof of the man's wicked words and ridiculous claims. The night's prophesy was nothing short of a *casus belli*, pitting Hanington against Peck, the lone horseman of his own illusory apocalypse.

Flexing his cramped fingers, William sat exhausted. He had been scribbling for hours. Disgusted to his core, Hanington collected his thoughts and his papers. Before Peck could inquire after it, Hanington pocketed the transcript of the evening's events and prepared to make his escape. His quarrel with Peck could wait. For now, it was more important to secrete the evidence to safety.

Hanington cast a last disparaging glance at his in-laws. They had much to discuss, but now was neither the time nor the place. Deeply disturbed by all he had witnessed, Hanington headed for the door. He could not wait to tell Mary what he had seen and heard. As he stepped into the gloaming, he very much doubted she would believe him.

Grist for the Mill

Jonathan Babcock [1]

On the heels of Hanington's hasty retreat, as the laity staggered dazed and disoriented into the night, Amos silently led his wife and daughter from the revival. His mind was reeling. His entire life Amos had sought evidence of God's favour, some token the Lord had not forsaken him. That sign was now manifest, yet the cost was unbearable: no less a price than his own flesh and blood. Having placed his faith in the hearsay of a pathological liar, Amos was undone. The *madnesse oblige* had reached the point of no return.

The Babcocks made their way home from Welling's house devoid of all thought and feeling. The revival had left them drained beyond repair, stony in the face of a bleak and uncertain future. Dusk had settled over the village — it was well past the dinner hour on February 13. As their heavy footfalls forged a fresh path through the snow, a single act suggests Amos was already concocting his plan. Despite the late hour, he headed for the home of his brother Jonathon.

Rousing the cabin's occupants, Amos drew Jonathon aside and asked his brother to help him mill some grain. Jonathon balked, pleading exhaustion. Amos pressed. Perhaps he convinced Jonathon he needed to expiate his shameful neglect of the cattle, the only excuse on offer that might render the task sufficiently urgent. Maybe he shared the chilling prophesy he had just witnessed. Whatever passed between the two brothers,

Amos's pleas eventually struck a chord. Jonathon agreed to help mill the grain, if only to gain a moment's peace.[2]

With Jonathon now in tow, the motley band marched on till at last they arrived at Amos's cabin. Shedding their winter coats, they set upon their charges. With their hands occupied, some small measure of normality descended over the room. Without a word, Dorcas settled the children into their bed for a fitful night's sleep. Amos went to the barn to fetch a sack of grain while Jonathon set up the gristmill, a cumbersome contraption of steel and stone. Machine at the ready, Jonathon poured a measure of the seed into the mill and began to turn the wheel. It was a graceless, thankless task.

While Jonathon milled and Dorcas puttered, Amos became increasingly erratic. Apropos of nothing, he abruptly began praying at the top of his lungs. Dorcas bade him to stop, fearing the din might rouse the children. Reproached, Amos grew petulant. He sat with a resounding thud — a parody of childlike innocence — removed his shoes and socks, and ran outside to stand in the snow. Oblivious to his impending frostbite, Amos gazed up at the heavens, sniffing the air like a bloodhound tracking a favoured scent.

Jonathon and Dorcas were dumbstruck. The prophesy was no doubt the cause of Amos's current dysphoria, yet it is possible Jonathon knew nothing of it. Jonathon went to the door, uncertain as to the proper course of action. Tentatively, he called to his brother as he would to a hysterical child. At Jonathon's urging, Amos returned to the cabin and sat down. But any sense of restored calm quickly evaporated. In grave and frantic tones, Amos whispered to Jonathon that "some great thing is going to happen tonight."[3]

Jonathon was vexed to his core. A desperate pleading glance to Dorcas went unanswered. Amos then declared: "the Lord should come to call the people to judgment."[4] Clearly, Amos had taken the preacher's declaration to heart. Jonathon, knowing Peck had made the same dire prediction countless times over the past weeks, dismissed the prophesy out of hand. Amos could not be placated, and the siblings were at a stalemate.

Another abrupt shift soon followed. Amos smiled and told Jonathon

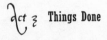

he "desired him to stop to pray for he was tired & sleepy,"[5] insisting Jonathon stay the night. Growing concerned for the family's safety, Jonathon reluctantly agreed. Like an excited child on Christmas morning, Amos ran upstairs to wake his children, insisting they tell Jonathon of their dreams. He pushed his daughter Dorcas to the fore. Perhaps he was looking for additional confirmation of the prophesy. In all likelihood, he had simply gone mad. Unnerved by her father's odd demeanour, Dorcas refused to speak. Without Peck's goading, she had nothing to say.

Jonathon paused, his hand resting on the mill, and stared at his brother. He was at a loss. For his part, Amos "appeared to be much distressed in his mind & Groaned often."[6] The situation was deteriorating rapidly.

As though struck by Divine inspiration, Amos became homiletic. Parables, Scripture, and verse flowed from his lips in a torrent, wild and ungoverned. He began to rant of "the Midnight Cry," an allusion to Matthew 25:6, in which Jesus — portrayed as a bridegroom — cries out in search of His companion, a common (if often misinterpreted) reference to Christ's calling His believers home. Amos sensed the Rapture was coming.

To keep his brother calm, Jonathon engaged him in conversation. Talk soon turned to visions and prophesies, as Amos recounted several of his own apocalyptic dreams. Fearing where such talk might lead, Jonathon invited his brother to join him in prayer. Amos leapt to his feet, pulled off his coat, and rolled up his shirt sleeves. He again ran out of doors. Resigned, Jonathon chose not to follow. Minutes passed. The children grew irritable and begged to return to bed.

Suddenly, Amos burst through the door. The room fell quiet, all silenced by a palpable sense of impending disaster. Circling to the table, Amos threw open the gristmill and took up a handful of ground meal. Glaring defiantly at his kin, he rubbed it over his arms and feet. As Judgment Day was at hand, there was no longer any reason to concern themselves with the needs of the flesh. Jonathon sat stoically, doing nothing to provoke a further outburst. Grabbing another handful of the coarse flour, Amos scattered it across the floor, shouting, "this is the bread of heaven."[7]

Then, as if drawn by some unheard noise, Amos again bolted through the cabin door and ran amok in the snow. Frozen and drenched to his bones, Amos called for Jonathon to bring him a towel. Jonathon grabbed some rough towelling and took it outside. He presented it to his brother, who secured it about his waist. Jonathon then left Amos to marvel at the night's starry vault and returned to the relative safety of the house.

Jonathon sat at the kitchen bench, his head in his hands. Through the doorway, Amos's raving continued unabated. At one point, Jonathan heard Amos cry out, "Oh Lord, not only my head and hands but my feet also."[8] Desperate for some semblance of sanity, Jonathon returned to the gristmill. Dorcas swept the scattered grain from the floor. For a brief, tantalizing moment, reason returned. It would not last. After an ominous silence, Amos again cried out, "I see the stars falling from heaven."[9]

With that, Amos made his way back toward the house.

actus reus [law Latin, "guilty act"]
A forbidden act; the wrongful deeds that
comprise the physical component of a crime.

End Times

Amos Babcock crossed the threshold of his house for the fourth and final time in the closing hours of February 13, 1805. He possessed a certainty and strength of will he had lacked his entire life. He was no longer Amos Babcock, a craven failure reliant on the charity of his betters to house his children. He was now an instrument of God, the Lord's right hand. At last keen of body, mind, and spirit, Amos stood ready to do His bidding. If God demanded a sacrifice, some penance for his pitiful life, it was not for Amos to question His wisdom.

Amos surveyed the room. His older children cowered snivelling against the wall, terrified to meet his eye. He summoned them to his side and arranged them by age along the kitchen bench. The eldest stiffened at his touch, standing locked in a military stance; the younger rested torpid on the bench, mercifully unaware of the gathering storm.

Amos gazed upon his family. Their eyes sought the floor, somnolent or fearful. Amos grabbed his wife by the shoulders, his face contorted in a manic grimace. "Be of good cheer,"[1] he implored her. It was all Dorcas could do to feign compliance. She forced a smile, if only for her children's sake. Amos followed her eye line, turning back to his offspring. In honeyed tones, Amos assured them nothing would harm them. He instructed them to pray and "to put their trust in God."[2] His words, aiming to comfort, fell wide of the mark. Having taken leave of his senses, Amos Babcock was no longer recognizable to his own kin.

Once again drawn by a noise he alone could hear, Amos went to the window and peered into the darkness. "I see them coming," he whispered, "it will be but a few minutes before they will be here."[3] The identity of the fast-approaching "they" remained an open question. Jonathon dared not speak or move, having just added paranoia to his brother's growing list of afflictions. Amos battened the shutters against the unseen enemy and paused to consider his options. He glanced around the room. Jonathon stood beside the gristmill. His wife and children remained fixed to the bench. His sister Mercy had silently joined them there. Seeing her, so close to his children, extinguished any lingering doubts. With new-found urgency, Amos set about his final preparations.

Crossing to the shelf were he kept his meagre collection of tools, Amos found a well-worn whetstone. From his vest pocket, he withdrew his knife, a folding blade seven inches in length. Cool and deliberate, he began methodically honing it on stone. Minutes passed as the slow, circular scraping grated on the nerves of the cabin's captive audience. Running his thumb along the freshly burnished steel, Amos marvelled at its edge. Holding it aloft for all to admire, Babcock exclaimed that the knife "was a Cross."[4] Reverently, he laid the knife and whetstone down on the hearth, arranging them in the shape of a crucifix. Then, as if in defiance of the Lord, he stomped on the knife and stone, sending them chattering across the floor.[5]

Righting himself, Amos crossed the room to stand before his eldest daughter, Dorcas. He reared back, spitting forcefully onto her forehead. Slowly, he began rubbing the spittle into her hair. As she cringed, he announced he was "anointing" her.[6] His face bore a look of pure menace, silencing any further protestations. He then moved down the line, repeating the grotesque sacrament with each child in turn. When he came to his sons, Henry and Caleb, he smiled as he administered his strange blessing, telling them they were now "Gideon's men."[7] As he reached the end of the line, spitting on his youngest child, Amos found himself face to face with Mercy. She stood, as always, a silent cipher. Pointedly, Amos turned and walked away. She was not anointed, a calculated slight.

His mind at last unmoored, Babcock lost all control, unleashing a fury

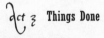

unthinkable only hours before. He grabbed his daughter, three-year-old Sarah, from her perch on the bench. The child fussed in his arms, pleading to be freed. Drawing a great breath, Amos blew with all his might into the child's mouth, choking her. As the child struggled for air, Amos held her aloft then hurled her across the room, her tiny body striking the jagged log wall. The sickening percussive thud as she hit the wall was immediately followed by an equally nauseating series of thumps as her head dragged down the course of logs before finally striking the floor. After an excruciating moment of silence, the child's fraught screams brought some small measure of relief to Dorcas and Jonathon. Though hurt, she was at least alive. As Sarah lay wailing, a crumpled mass of blood and bedclothes, no one dared go to her aid. Amos's wife wept, paralyzed by fear and rage.

His wrath unbound, Amos spun toward Mercy. He pulled off his sister's hat and ordered her to remove her shoes and "make herself ready."[8] Mercy complied, falling to her knees, her face an impassive mask.

Pacing wildly, hunched and tortured, Amos stopped short, pulled himself up to his full height and retrieved his knife. Lifting his head, his arms outstretched in a mockery of the Crucifixion, Amos proclaimed he was the Angel Gabriel and declared that the day of reckoning was at hand. As he lowered his heaven-fixed gaze, he confronted Dorcas, demanding his wife stare into his eyes. Searching his face and seeing no sign of the man she once knew, Dorcas averted her eyes. Knife at the ready, he threatened her time and again, screaming that if she dared look away, he "would run her through."[9] Dorcas looked away, unable to stare boldfaced into madness. He struck her hard with his fist without hesitation and the backhanded blow sent Dorcas reeling, howling in shock and anguish.

In this new world gone mad, his wife's pain delighted Amos. Spurred by a sudden change in the weather, Babcock began to dance about the room. The silver in his hand caught the light, and for a moment he was mesmerized, transfixed by his own reflection in the blade's polished face. At last tearing himself from his febrile revelry, Amos commanded Jonathon to strip and prepare himself to die. Tempting fate, Jonathon refused. After several menacing thrusts of the knife, Jonathon finally acquiesced.

Jonathon's capitulation was a feint, a ruse designed to stall for time.

Minutes passed as the brothers stood locked in a battle of wills. Enraged by his sibling's reticence, Amos ordered Jonathon "in the name of the Lord God of Israel"[10] to bow. When Jonathon balked, Amos petulantly repeated he was the Angel Gabriel — the desperate tantrum of a lethal toddler. Trusting that compliance might restore a modicum of sanity, Jonathon reluctantly did as directed. Stripped bare and resigned, he knelt before his brother.

Fuelled by unseen demons, Amos's mental state grew ever more precarious. He vacillated wildly between giddy jubilation and mordant despondency. One moment he berated himself and others for their sins, the next he burst into song, dancing about the kitchen, gibbering incoherently. His face alternately bore traces of rapture and lunacy.

In the midst of a manic jig, the last remaining tether of reason in Amos Babcock's head snapped. Without warning, he lunged across the room, burying his knife up to the hilt into his sister's chest.[11] Tugging out the blade, Amos wheeled back and struck again. With a sweeping arc, he sliced open the back of Mercy's head. The blade skittered across her skull, severing her scalp and unleashing a torrent of blood. As she fell to the floor, Amos repositioned himself astride her convulsing torso. Calmly, he took the blade, and with a flick of the wrist, he slashed open her stomach, disembowelling her.

Mercy "screeched out"[12] in agony, drew a last laboured breath, then was gone.

Act 3 Things Done

act 4
Deconstructing History

Raising the Alarm

It is at this very moment, with Mercy's last breath, that history and popular culture diverge. Fact and fiction part company, destined to share only a passing acquaintance from here on out. In the epic saga of the killing of Mercy Hall, media accounts of what happened in the aftermath of the murder took on a life all their own, one built of half-truths, conjecture, and narrative devices designed to titillate, if not inform.

The myth-building began as Mercy's lifeless body fell to the floor. In his 1898 treatise, William Reynolds claimed Jonathon Babcock was not spurred into action until he "saw the blood flow."[1] The image of Jonathon kneeling motionless as Mercy lay dying was repeated without challenge in every subsequent reworking of the story, each account ratcheting up the violence and revelling in the sanguinary portrait.

In truth, Jonathon never saw any blood. By his own account, Jonathon only saw Amos approach Mercy with the knife, at which point Jonathon fled for help. As he ran, he "heard the Deceased Screech out."[2] Jonathon never witnessed Amos stab his sister, nor did he know she was dead when he bolted from the cabin.

The misinformation campaign continued with erroneous reports of where Jonathon went during his desperate flight from the scene of the crime. Again, comparisons of original witness testimony and all popular depictions reveal serious discrepancies and more than a little poetic

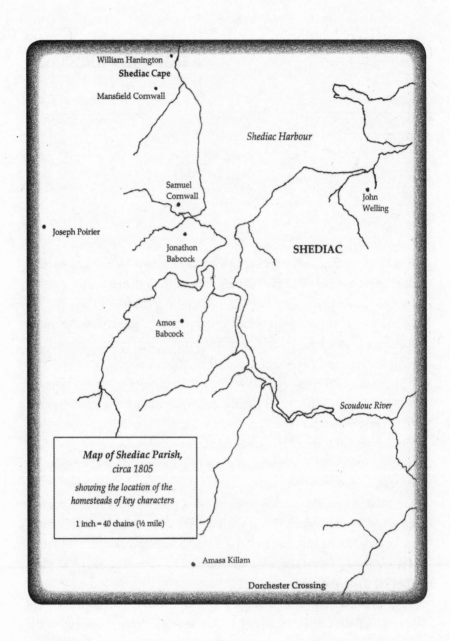

William Hanington

Shediac Cape

Mansfield Cornwall

Shediac Harbour

Samuel
Cornwall

John
Welling

Joseph Poirier

Jonathon
Babcock

SHEDIAC

Amos
Babcock

Scoudouc River

*Map of Shediac Parish,
circa 1805*

*showing the location of the
homesteads of key characters*

1 inch = 40 chains (½ mile)

Amasa Killam

Dorchester Crossing

licence. Jonathon's inquest testimony states that after he ran from Amos's house, he "Alarmed the Neighbours."[3] Which neighbours he alarmed were never specified. According to Reynolds and his fellow raconteurs, Jonathon ran to the closest house, that of the Acadian Joseph Poirier. There, in the gospel according to Reynolds et al., Jonathon was given clothing to cover his still-naked body. From Poirier's house, Babcock then made his way to the home of William Hanington, "where he aroused the inmates by crying and shouting that his brother Amasa had stabbed his sister."[4]

A number of problems are inherent in Reynolds's sequence of events, however, not least of which is Jonathon's calling his brother by the wrong name. To reconstruct Jonathon's panicked midnight run through Shediac Parish, it is helpful to understand the spatial relationships among the various households.[5]

§

If Jonathon had in fact fled Amos's cabin with little if any clothing in the dead of a New Brunswick winter's eve, it defies logic that he ran to the home of Joseph Poirier — a considerable distance away — rather than to his own, much closer house, where he was certain to find clothes. Rational arguments aside, Reynolds's oft-mimicked version of Jonathon's mad dash directly contradicts other eyewitness accounts from that night — specifically that of William Hanington.

According to Hanington, he neither saw nor spoke to Jonathon Babcock on the night of the murder. On the contrary, Hanington claimed he learned of Mercy's death from none other than Jacob Peck. Hanington, in a letter to a local magistrate hours after the killing, states, "a Jacob Peck & Mansfield Cornwall came to my house about one Hour Before Day Light to let me know that Amos Babcock had Murdered his Sister."[6] Hanington then describes, in excessive and sometimes exhausting detail, exactly what transpired that evening. Not once does he mention Jonathon Babcock.

Hanington's revelation raises an immediate and troubling question: how did Jacob Peck know of the murder so quickly? Three possible explanations warrant consideration. The first is that Peck was present in Babcock's home when the murder occurred. The evangelist was with Amos in the hours before the killing, and it is conceivable he travelled with him to Amos's house following the revival and there witnessed the murder. However, no witness statements or even second-hand accounts place Peck at the murder scene. An alternate interpretation is that Peck knew of Amos's intent to kill his sister and took it upon himself to warn the town elders. Again, though possible, this option is improbable. According to Hanington's testimony, Peck informed him the deed was done, not that it was imminent or likely. The final, and most plausible, explanation is that Jonathon ran to John Welling's home, the platform for Peck's incendiary revival. There, he found Peck, who in turn went to rouse William Hanington.

Given the animosity brewing between Peck and Hanington, it is curious the preacher agreed to serve as messenger. It stands to reason Peck was coerced into summoning the town elder by his fellow revivalists, rather than electing to go of his own accord. Mansfield Cornwall, Hanington's nearest neighbour, likely joined Peck to guide him to Hanington's home in Shediac Cape. Hanington's letter noted that Amasa Killam — also in attendance at the revival — accompanied Peck and Cornwall to his house, lending further credibility to the final scenario.

That William Hanington was wrenched from his sleep by Jacob Peck rather than by Jonathon Babcock also highlights another key misconception in the popular record. In his 1915 rendition of the crime, Joseph Lawrence reported that Jonathon shouted to the Hanington household that Amos had stabbed his sister.[7] Lawrence claimed that in response, "Mr. Hanington told him he was as guilty as his brother."[8] Unlike the bulk of Lawrence's account, this particular detail was not drawn from Reynolds's 1898 article, which never mentioned Hanington's reply. Although straying from the Reynolds party line, Lawrence did not fabricate the exchange out of whole cloth; he merely misinterpreted a tidbit buried in the archival record.

William Hanington's reply comes from an interview his oldest surviving son, William Jr., gave in his dotage. Junior was ten years old at the time of Mercy's murder and recalled laying in the bedroom next to his parents on the night in question. According to Will Jr., after the house was awakened with the news of Mercy's death, he remembered hearing his father tell the messenger that he was as guilty as Amos for the crime.[9] Following the publication of Reynolds's article in 1898 and the erroneous report that Jonathon had alarmed the house that night, the editors of Lawrence's posthumous book (most likely W.O. Raymond) mistakenly assumed Hanington had directed his damning accusation at Jonathon Babcock, when in fact it was Jacob Peck whom Hanington had castigated. The incident remains one in a series of miscommunications in which Hanington's suspicions of the itinerant preacher were lost in translation, both at the time of the murder and ever since.

Equally curious are the reasons the storytellers give for the need all involved felt to notify William Hanington. John Belliveau, in his 2003 history of Shediac, states that Hanington was "a sort of clerk of the peace, 'chairman of the quorum', a local magistrate."[10] Not a single word of truth resides in the claim. The highest offices Hanington held at that time were Surveyor of Roads and Collector for the District of Dorchester,[11] neither of which bestowed him with any jurisdictional authority over criminal activity. Without question, he was neither a magistrate nor even "sort of" a clerk of the peace. Shediac was not officially declared a parish until 1825[12] and, as such, could not appoint its own constables, magistrates, or justices of the peace at the time of the killing. Hanington was, at best, a town elder, a rather nebulous designation lacking in any real power.

His formal rank notwithstanding, Hanington was a prosperous land-owner and merchant, and he had resided in the area longer than any other English-speaking settler. A calm, mature, and rational man, he seemed to all to be the obvious choice in such extraordinary circumstances. For want of anyone better qualified, the task of dealing with the first murder ever committed in the district fell to William Hanington.

Appointed detective by proclamation if not by affirmation, Hanington got off to a rocky start. Fearing Amos's murderous rage would continue, driving him to kill his wife and children, Hanington thought there was little time to spare. Clad only in his nightshirt, Hanington instructed

Peck, Killam, and Cornwall to go to "the french people" (presumably the family of Joseph Poirier) and insist they accompany the men to Babcock's house to detain him. [13]

Clearly Jacob Peck had other plans. Disregarding Hanington's directive, the preacher instead led his two associates to the nearby home of Mansfield Cornwall, where they remained for the rest of the evening. When pressed, Peck claimed they had gone to Cornwall's to wait for Hanington. As Hanington was unaware of the change in plan, the men never regrouped. Peck had purposefully waylaid the rescue party, either to avoid Hanington, who had just accused him of being complicit in the murder, or to sidestep an encounter with Amos Babcock. Peck had no way of knowing what Babcock might say once apprehended, and the preacher correctly deduced it was best not to be in the room should Babcock start talking.

In the meantime, William Hanington dressed and began the arduous trek to the home of Joseph Poirier. It was hard going, with bottomless snowbanks and impassable roads. Hanington, outfitted with his snowshoes, was forced to venture across the ice of Shediac Harbour.

Hanington's decision to enlist the Acadians was odd, given that he already had Peck, Killam, and Cornwall. The chasm rent by language and culture ran deep, dividing the French and English communities despite their proximity. Each group kept largely to its own. Still, Hanington recognized he needed considerable muscle to bring the murderous Babcock under control. Without the French, all he had was intellectual might. Hanington and Cornwall were gentleman farmers, having risen to the enviable position of employing others to do the heavy lifting. Jacob Peck, desperately aspiring to the gentrified class, was not the least bit physically imposing. Worse still, Peck was, to his core, a cowardly interloper with no real ties to the community. Were violence to erupt, Hanington had little faith the preacher would risk life or limb. Amos Babcock, on the other hand, was of formidable mettle, made all the more dangerous by virtue of the knife. The Poiriers were hale and hardy yeomen, well able to take down Babcock should he put up a fight.

Hanington arrived at the Poirier homestead in the darkest hour before dawn. He was dismayed to discover Peck and the others were nowhere to be found. Despite all media claims to the contrary, there was also no sign of Jonathon Babcock.

Having roused the poor people from their beds, Hanington shared what he knew of the murder with the startled Poiriers. Hanington — garrulous at the best of times and prone to glossolalia in times of high excitement — droned on at length. Having exhausted his tale and the patience of his hosts, Hanington at last came to the reason for his late-night intrusion. William wanted Joseph's two largest sons, Peter and Joseph Jr., to accompany him to Babcock's home and help subdue the murderous blackguard. Keen to partake in the drama, the boys agreed, quickly strapping on their snowshoes and bounding out the door. With the necessary reinforcements secured, Hanington and the two hulking Poiriers marched east, through the darkness toward the unknown.

The Arrest

For all the histrionics that preceded it, the actual capture and arrest of Amos Babcock was decidedly bathetic. Hanington described the scene as he and his French muscle burst into Babcock's home:

> I found the prisoner standing upright & his wife & children seated in a row. As he had no arms I immediately seized & we bound him. As soon as he was secured I asked his wife if her sister was dead. She said she was. I then made no further enquiry untill [sic] the English people arrived — which I believe was something more than half an hour.[1]

Though scant in detail, Hanington's testimony faithfully recalled the events in question, favouring fidelity over pomp. Today, it remains the sole surviving first-hand account of Babcock's capture.

Ninety-three years after the fact, the episode received an extraneous injection of drama courtesy of William Reynolds. In his seminal 1898 article, Reynolds offers up a far more stirring and detailed account of Amos's arrest, including direct quotes not drawn from Hanington's witness statement. Reynolds picks up the scene as Hanington and the Poiriers arrive at Babcock's home:

On entering the house where the tragedy had been committed, they found Amasa Babcock walking about with his hands clasped. Mr. Hanington told the Poirier brothers to seize him. Babcock resisted and asked what they were going to do. Their reply was that they intended to hold him a prisoner, whereupon he cried out "Gideon's men, arise!" On hearing these words, his two young sons, Caleb and Henry, jumped up as if to assist him, but were compelled to sit down again, and the prisoner was secured. The body of Mercy Hall was not in the house, nor was it then known where it had been placed. When Mrs. Babcock was asked if her sister-in-law was dead, she simply said "yes".[2]

If Reynolds's quotes are accurate, the images they evoke would be comical were it not for the tragic circumstance. Babcock's entreating his gangling sons—Henry, fourteen, and Caleb, eleven—to rise up against the strapping Poiriers reveals his level of delusion and desperation. That the boys were "compelled to sit down again" is something of an understatement.

Both Hanington's first-hand and Reynolds's embellished accounts agree on two key facts: Amos was unarmed when the men arrived, and Babcock's wife responded to Hanington's inquiry about Mercy's death. There are also important discrepancies between the two versions. For example, Hanington claimed he seized Babcock, while in Reynolds's version it was the Poiriers who tackled the raving outlaw.

Reynolds continues, recounting the events immediately following Babcock's arrest:

The prisoner, with his arms securely strapped, was taken to Mr. Hanington's house. While there he kept repeating, 'Aha! Aha! Aha! It was permitted! It was permitted!' The statement of Jonathon Babcock was written down, and the necessary papers were prepared to authorize a commitment to prison. On seeing the papers, Amasa shouted, 'There are letters to Damascus! Send them to Damascus!' It was evident that he was thinking of Saul's persecution of the Christians.[3]

Liberally seasoned with details and quotes not found elsewhere in the public record, the veracity of Reynolds's account must be called into question as the information it presents has no identified source. Furthermore, the passage includes at least one significant error. Reynolds claims Jonathon Babcock's statement was taken immediately following the murder, during the early morning hours of February 14, but the statement was not written until six days later, on February 20, when Jonathon was deposed during the coroner's inquest. Nowhere do court records hint that Jonathon gave more than one statement.[4] All existing statements by Hanington indicate he never encountered Jonathon Babcock on the night of the murder, much less deposed him. As for "the necessary papers...to authorize a commitment to prison," Reynolds's article contains the first and only mention of such items. No one present, including Hanington, had the authority to create such documents, rendering this lone account of their creation suspect.

Inconsistencies and provenance aside, Reynolds well understood the demands of character and plot development, and the quotes he introduces are compelling. Amos's supposed allusions to Saul, Acts 9:2, and the letters to Damascus hint at Babcock's considerable knowledge of Scripture as well as his growing paranoia and feelings of persecution. Babcock no doubt felt a kinship with Saul, another convert to preaching who faced his own ruinous conflicts with non-believers. As for Amos's assertion that the killing "was permitted," that contention would later form the basis of his legal defence.

While Amos raved of Damascus and justifiable homicide, the search for Mercy's body proceeded with all due haste. As the morning of February 14 dawned, the residents of Shediac Parish had little time for thoughts of unrequited love or winged Cupids. News of the bloody events at the Babcock home spread unchecked through the tiny hamlet. Male representatives from every English household in the district arrived at first light, united in a single mission: to find the body of the victim, Mercy Hall.

Details of the search efforts are scant in the archives. William Hanington noted that Amasa Killam and Simeon Jenks headed the search party.[5] As an afterthought, Hanington closed one letter to Justice William Black with the postscript, "I forgot to mention he had dragged the body of the deceased out of his house and buried it in the snow."[6] It was in that frozen tomb, only yards from the cabin, that the searchers discovered what remained of Mercy Babcock Hall.

The aftermath of Mercy's killing was unquestionably a chaotic and ill-documented time. As the village reeled in shock and disbelief, few had occasion to record the events for posterity. In the decades that followed, storytellers would test the boundaries of historical biography, at times sacrificing accuracy to the gods of yellow journalism.

Lost amid all the revelations, overworked rhetoric, and questionable sources is another contemporaneous and far more significant development in the story. As Amos thundered and the townsfolk searched, no one noticed as Jacob Peck quietly took his leave of Shediac Parish, never to return.

The Abyss

At the edge of ancient maps, cartographers scrawled, "here, there be dragons,"[2] warning those who would venture beyond that they were delving into uncharted and dangerous waters. In the odyssey of Babcock and Peck, we have reached the edge of the known world and are teetering over an abyss in the historical record guarded by a lone but cunning dragon: William Kilby Reynolds. That Reynolds himself was the cause of the archival void only compounds the peril.

To know best how to proceed, we must first understand how time, tides, and the frailties of men have conspired to form the gap. By the time the criminal trial of Amos Babcock drew to a close in the waning months of 1805, the official written record of the case was extensive. It included witness statements from the key players, reports from the coroner's inquest, the court minutes and associated documents, and a lone June 1805 media report detailing the trial and its outcome. At first, the official case documents were kept in the courthouse, but as the years passed, personnel came and went, space grew tight, and the files changed hands and location. Those directly involved grew old and died, and the case seemed destined for the historical scrap heap. Then, late in the nineteenth century, the story caught the attention of a man named Joseph W. Lawrence.

Lawrence was the newly elected president of the recently formed New Brunswick Historical Society.[3] Acclaimed as "a speaker of more than ordinary ability,"[4] Lawrence gave annual presentations to the society on a variety of topics he hoped might be of interest to its growing membership. In August 1884, Joseph Lawrence delivered a riveting lecture on the Babcock tragedy. The talk was well received, shocking a capacity crowd in Saint John with its graphic depictions of the brutal crime and eliciting heated debate regarding the tale's controversial religious overtones. As no copies of the address survive, the sources or documents Lawrence referenced are unknown.

Typically, such lectures were published, either by the society or in the local newspaper, but Lawrence had other plans for this particular story. He was writing a book on the province's nascent judicial system and the men who served as its overseers, tentatively entitled *The Judges of New Brunswick and Their Times*. Lawrence planned to feature the Babcock tale in the chapter on its presiding judge. As fate would have it, Joseph Lawrence died suddenly on November 6, 1892, months short of completing the work. Recognizing the importance of the project, Alfred August Stockton — a lawyer and politician of considerable repute and a long-time admirer of Lawrence — agreed to edit and complete the book in Joseph's honour.

In the meantime, Lawrence's 1884 talk reignited interest in the strange happenings in Shediac Parish. William K. Reynolds, a fellow New Brunswick historian, was in the final stages of his latest endeavour: a new magazine focused on issues relevant to the Maritimes. Reynolds, also based in Saint John, served as the journal's editor, publisher, and chief contributor.[5] Reynolds had heard the rekindled gossip about Babcock and Peck, the metaphysical magician whose riotous revivals sparked the killing. Since it had not yet been published, Reynolds wanted to include Lawrence's lecture in the inaugural July–December issue of *New Brunswick Magazine* but, after a lengthy series of inquiries, discovered it was un- available for print. Still, Reynolds remained captivated by the story, and elected to write his own version. For reasons known only to him, Reynolds chose to publish the article under the pseudonym "Roslynde." Since most of the magazine's first issue was authored by Reynolds, the pseudonym might have been little more than a vain attempt at diversity.

The article is completely devoid of citations or references. Of his sources, Reynolds says only: "Through the aid of Rev. W.O. Raymond, however, the information upon which Mr. Lawrence based his paper has been secured, and with some additional facts, the story is now told in more complete form than on the occasion in question."[6] Careful review of the text, however, reveals the identity of four of Reynolds's primary sources: a newspaper account in the June 1805 *Royal Gazette* and the witness statements of three key players — Dorcas Babcock, Amasa Killam, and William Hanington. Identifying the authors of the witness statements was a matter of deductive reasoning, matching specific details or quotes in the article to the person or persons present when the incidents occurred.

Although entertaining, Reynolds's article is an uneven mix, providing copious particulars for certain anecdotes while offering only vague or imprecise descriptions of other pivotal events. This might well be an artifact of the sources themselves. For the specifics of the murder, Reynolds relies on Dorcas's statement. For events leading up to and including Babcock's arrest, he uses the words of William Hanington.[7] Amasa Killam's statement presumably contained details of Amos's fateful journey to the jail in Dorchester. Reynolds mentions the trial only in passing — what little he includes comes directly from the brief newspaper account — and takes scant notice of Jacob Peck. Equally apparent is that Reynolds did not have access to the material currently residing in the public archives, including the court records, coroner's inquest, and all other extant witness statements. Many of these accounts conflict with Reynolds's article, if not refuting it outright.

Why Reynolds chose those particular witness statements is unclear, as is how they came to be culled from the other evidentiary materials in the case.[8] How Reynolds gained possession of the statements is far easier to trace. In the article, he graciously acknowledges the assistance of the Reverend William Obder Raymond, who had a well-documented connection to Lawrence that clearly worked in Reynolds's favour.

When Joseph Lawrence's manuscript was forwarded to A.A. Stockton for completion, the preface of the book notes, "there remained much for Dr. Stockton to do."[9] As the century drew to a close and Stockton fell ill, the work had progressed only as far as Chapter Sixteen. W.O. Raymond, himself a historian and writer of some note, volunteered to complete the book and deliver it to the publisher.[10] Accordingly, Lawrence's extensive collection of research materials passed from Stockton to Raymond. When pressed by Reynolds for materials in the Babcock case, Raymond no doubt forwarded whatever sources he found among Lawrence's notes. How Joseph Lawrence first came by the evidentiary witness statements — deemed government property — is unknown, although his tenure as historical society president undoubtedly greased the rails.[11]

The Raymond connection leads us to another perplexing twist in the popular record. Joseph Lawrence wrote and delivered the original lecture on Babcock in 1884, then died in 1892. Yet, in his book published post-humously in 1915, the Babcock section included in Chapter Five is an almost verbatim reprint of Reynolds's 1898 article, save for a few minor revisions. All this begs the question: who plagiarized whom? Had Raymond simply given Reynolds a copy of Lawrence's original talk — or perhaps a draft of the relevant section of the manuscript of *The Judges of New Brunswick and Their Times* — which Reynolds then published verbatim? Or did Raymond insert the Reynolds article into the manuscript before submitting it for publication? Admittedly, in the years before stringent copyright laws, there was less concern for credited authorship, yet the question remains: who actually wrote the seminal, if somewhat erroneous, version of the Babcock story from which all subsequent accounts have been drawn — Reynolds or Lawrence? Perhaps the reason Reynolds published the piece under a pseudonym was to acknowledge that its true authorship was dubious.

Paper shuffles among historians notwithstanding, the sad outcome of the story is that the original witness statements by Dorcas Babcock, Amasa Killam, and William Hanington have been lost in the century since either Lawrence or Reynolds last held them. That the statements once existed is irrefutable — they were specifically noted in the report from the coroner's inquest, as well as in documentation relating to the first grand jury empanelled in the case. Equally certain is that the statements are no longer part of the permanent record of the case and no copies are retained in any public archive. They are not among the papers donated to the New Brunswick Museum Archives as part of the William Kilby Reynolds Collection, nor can they be found in either the Lawrence or Raymond Fonds. The statements are also not among the artifacts contained in the J.W. Lawrence, Dr. A.A. Stockton, or W.O. Raymond notebooks at the Library and Archives of Canada. The last known location of all three documents was the hands of William Kirby Reynolds.

As a consequence, Reynolds's account is a double-edged sword. To the good, it remains the sole source of information regarding key segments of the story. It is also the last surviving glimpse of the now-lost witness statements of Dorcas Babcock and Amasa Killam. To the bad, there is the loss of those statements from the public record, likely through the action (or inaction) of Reynolds. The vital information they contained effectively has been erased. Only those few snippets Reynolds deemed worthy of note endure.

Such is the nature of this particular dragon. To dismiss Reynolds's account outright would be to lose the only available reference. Indirect evidence from other sources corroborates at least some of the information in Reynolds's article, lending the account limited credibility. To accept it without condition, however, is equally troubling, as comparisons to original sources reveal the article is riddled with inaccuracies, errors (such as consistently referring to Amos as "Amasa"), and often overt contradictions to extant witness testimony. As with all media reports, Reynolds's version of events must be approached with caution and a healthy degree of skepticism.

Such is the ephemeral nature of the historical record. Time's arrow has claimed crucial evidence in the saga of Amos, Jacob, and Mercy. What traces remain cannot always be trusted. If the capture and arrest of Amos Babcock exposed a gaping hole in the case's archive, popular accounts of what happened next reveal a chasm only fabulists dared traverse.

Damages

Amasa Killam[1]

Following Babcock's "arrest" by Hanington and the Poiriers, Hanington's eyewitness account ends abruptly, creating a line of demarcation in the official documentation of the case. The account was written just after dawn on February 14, 1805, while Amos Babcock sat bound in Hanington's house.[2] The historical record then falls maddeningly silent for one week. The next irrefutable evidence comes on February 20, when the coroner notes that Babcock was "strongly ironed in the dungeon" in Dorchester.[3] The surviving archival record, however, contains nothing about how Amos Babcock went from Shediac Parish to Dorchester, how long the journey lasted, or what might have happened along the way. Reynolds casts the lone light on this period:

> Babcock was then taken to the house of Amasa Killam, who had been one of those prominent in the revival. There the prisoner became more violent in his insanity, and to restrain him he was placed upon a bed with his arms pinioned and fastened down to the floor. The weather was then very stormy, and traveling, in the primitive condition of the roads of those days, was out of the question. By the third day after the tragedy, however, the storm had abated, and several men of the neighbourhood started out to take Babcock to prison.

Putting straps on his arms, they placed him on a light one-horse sled, and putting on their snow-shoes they hauled him by hand through the woods to the county jail at Dorchester, a distance of some twenty-six miles. Truly, one of the strangest winter journeys ever made in the wilderness of this country.[4]

While Reynolds's description remains suspect, its credibility far exceeds those that followed. Perhaps it is because this portion of the story is so thinly sourced and speculative that subsequent chroniclers of the tale felt free to take such creative licence. These revisionist yarns would be comical if they did not profess to be historically accurate works of non-fiction.

The revamping of Babcock's odyssey begins slowly and with some subtlety. The 1915 account in *The Judges of New Brunswick* is, of course, a literal reprint of Reynolds's article.[5] Time and tastes change, and thirteen years later John Clarence Webster — in his much-lauded *History of Shediac, New Brunswick* — opted to spice up this particular anecdote. He deleted the trip to Amasa Killam's outright, along with the three-day delay and the storm, and added a new twist: "on the way, he broke loose but was recaptured."[6] What source, if any, was the basis for this strange new addition can no longer be found among Webster's otherwise exhaustive research notes for the book.[7]

Regardless of the questionable provenance of Babcock's escape, it clearly caught the eye of John Belliveau, who not only includes it in his 2003 account but limns it with his own playful details: "once, when the sled overturned, Babcock broke his bonds and escaped, but only momentarily."[8] B.J. Grant, too, elected to rewrite history in his 1983 version of the event. Grant does away with the escape, brings back the drama of the impending storm, but then alters the team's motivation for stopping at Killam's house. According to Grant, it was not the worsening weather but rather a "fit" by Babcock, brought on by their approach to Killam's house — "the home of another of those who'd been 'revivalled'" — that forced the party to a halt.[9] Twenty years later, crime writer Allison Finnamore transmuted the tale again, reworking Grant's version and discounting all others that came before. Like Grant, Finnamore credits a "religious fit," not bad weather, with bringing the journey to a halt.[10] But Finnamore cannot resist adding her own take on events. She reinserts Hanington into the jail-bound crew, along with the Poirier brothers, but does away with the supposed escape attempt, stating "the rest of the trip was uneventful."[11]

Poetic licence and narrative devices aside, these fictionalized accounts of Babcock's voyage to the Dorchester jail do the story a grave disservice in that they distract from one of the key players in the saga: Amasa Killam.

Amasa Killam was born in Nova Scotia in 1771, the first son of Amasa Killam Sr. and Elizabeth Emerson. At the turn of the century, Amasa Jr. headed north to try his hand at farming in New Brunswick. To better his lot in life, he twice petitioned for land in Westmorland County — including once with his friend and neighbour Amos Babcock — but was denied at every turn.[12] Killam was destined to be a landless yeoman for the remainder of his days. Unlucky in land, Amasa had better fortune with affairs of the heart. He met and married a local girl, Sarah Sanford. Despite the couple's humble circumstances, one of their offspring — Amasa Emerson Killam — was later elected to New Brunswick's Legislative Assembly. By all accounts, Amasa Killam was a humble, decent man, a hard-working crofter and devout Baptist. He lacked material wealth but had earned the respect of his neighbours with his integrity and strong work ethic.

On account of his standing in the community, his friendship with Amos Babcock, and his geographic proximity, Amasa Killam alone bore witness to every aspect of what Reynolds terms the "Babcock Tragedy." He was among the first Shediac villagers to meet Jacob Peck, making the preacher's acquaintance within hours of Peck's arrival. Killam also attended every revival Peck held in the parish, hosting at least one of the unconventional rituals in his own home. He was among the first to learn of the murder the night it occurred, accompanying Peck and Cornwall to inform Hanington of the crime. Killam played a major role in the search for Mercy's body, and he served on the coroner's inquest jury, standing front and centre at her autopsy. Killam's home served as a makeshift jail for the dangerously unstable Amos Babcock, who reportedly spent three days harnessed to his floor. And Amasa Killam would be called to give testimony in the criminal proceedings for both Amos Babcock and Jacob Peck. Yet, for all this, Reynolds reduces Amasa Killam to a minor player, and few of the tale's subsequent scribes mention him at all. Killam warrants far more attention than he has been afforded, and the loss of his written statement leaves a significant hole in the evidentiary record of the case.

That loss resonates beyond the matter of *The Crown v. Amos Babcock*. Reynolds pays little heed to the role of Jacob Peck in Mercy's murder and gives no notice to the criminal proceedings against Peck that followed. The statements of Amasa Killam, William Hanington, and Dorcas Babcock held significant references to Peck that Reynolds dismisses as inconsequential; Reynolds mined their accounts only for what they contained about Babcock. Certainly, all three witnesses were well-acquainted with Peck's behaviour and actions in the weeks leading up to the killing, and their observations would have contributed greatly to our understanding of the preacher's legal culpability in the murder.

Having negotiated the dragon and crossed the Rubicon of a media-born facsimile of history, we once again plant our feet firmly on the solid ground of the legitimate archival record.

Act 5

The Preamble

malingering To feign illness or injury in order to escape punishment or gain compensation.

Dorchester

Robert Keillor [1]

Robert Keillor was something of a drinking man.[2] One of his two chosen professions — tavern owner[3] — certainly made it easy for him to indulge. His tendency toward drunkenness, however, was at odds with his second profession — jailer at the Dorchester Courthouse. Resourceful and clever, Keillor successfully combined his seemingly disparate careers thanks to a quirk of geography. Robert's tavern was housed inside the courthouse, one floor above its basement jail. Such proximity no doubt reduced the commuting time between his two posts.

In defence of the good people of Dorchester, who likely would have not placed a drunk in such a key position of authority (two key positions, some might argue), his brother John had, for all intents and purposes, bought the job for Robert. To understand why, we first need to understand the Keillors.

The family hailed from Skelton-in-Cleveland in England's idyllic Yorkshire Dales, where Robert was born on September 9, 1764.[4] Robert, brother John, and the rest of the Keillor clan emigrated to the New World in 1774. Their father, a stonemason by trade, purchased a small plot of land near Fort Cumberland in Nova Scotia. In 1782 John Keillor left the family home and moved north to the Parish of Dorchester. He petitioned for and won two hundred and fifty acres of land in the parish and encouraged his brothers Robert and Thomas to do likewise. John's siblings were also awarded land, which John promptly purchased from them for pence on the acre.[5]

Naive and somewhat malleable, Robert often did as John suggested; sometimes, he simply did as John did. When John told Robert to move to Dorchester, Robert complied. When John married the daughter of a prominent Yorkshire family, a girl by the name of Elizabeth Weldon, Robert promptly married her sister Ann, tying the knot on December 10, 1792.[6] They never had children.

Where the brothers diverged, however, was in their respective ambitions. Robert was a hopeless parvenu, trapped at the losing end of a lopsided filial embrace. Left to his own devices, Robert wanted nothing more than a simple life for himself and contemplated taking up farming or stonemasonry, like his father before him. John had far grander dreams. He aspired to enter the rarefied stratum of the social elite by becoming a justice of the peace. To that end, John married well, the daughter of a renowned judge. Then, in 1801, as luck would have it, the old courthouse and jail for Westmorland County burned to the ground. Where others saw a civic tragedy, John saw opportunity.[7]

John Keillor's land holdings had grown to include all of what is now the village of Dorchester proper. In a bid to secure his place in the gentrified class, John agreed to donate four acres of land in a prime location — at the crossroads between Saint John and Nova Scotia — for the county to build the new courthouse. In the deed bestowing the land to the county, Keillor said he made his generous gift "in consideration of the good will I have for the County of Westmorland and the desire I feel to promote the interests and advancement thereof."[8] Keillor's motives, however, were not entirely altruistic. The grant afforded him considerable sway in the courthouse's construction and operation. As such, it seemed only fitting that the coveted role of jailer would fall to his brother Robert, along with the highly lucrative licence to operate a tavern conveniently located on its ground floor.

In Robert's defence, he was not wholly unsuited for the job. He had served as constable for Dorchester for one year (1799),[9] giving him some small experience in law enforcement. His leap to jailer, though unquestionably driven by his brother's ambitions, was not, as it appeared to many, an unmitigated act of nepotism.

It was therefore into Robert's capable, if sometimes shaky, hands as jailer that the struggling and delusional figure of Amos Babcock was delivered on a frigid morning in February 1805. Keillor left Babcock "strongly ironed in the dungeon,"[10] sharing the cell with a local horse thief and burglar named John Jerome.

Robert's stint as jailer might have relegated him to a minor role in the Babcock saga, but something he saw in the course of his duties would soon propel him centre stage. Shortly after Keillor shackled Amos in the jail, he witnessed something — an "accidental discovery"[11] — that the prosecution later would argue proved beyond a shadow of a doubt that Amos Babcock was not insane but merely acting crazy in the hope of avoiding punishment for his crime. Robert's sharp, if somewhat bloodshot, eye made him a key witness in the trial of Amos Babcock, leading many to argue he helped send a mentally unstable man to his death.

corpus delicti [Latin, "body of the crime"]
The material substance on which a crime has been
committed; the physical evidence of a crime, such
as the corpse of a murdered person.

Charnel House

Gideon Palmer [1]

The smell was inescapable, a funk that clouded the air, permeating the walls and their clothes. A cloying, oily entity melding rot and despair that tattooed their skin. The stench emanated from the kitchen, where the body of Mercy Hall rested, awaiting its fate. Joseph Poirier, the Acadian neighbour entrusted to keep her remains pending a formal investigation, enlisted the help of his brothers — Pascal and Chrysosten — to move her from the root cellar where she had rested to prevent decay. What remained of Mercy Hall now lay, coiled and frozen, on the Poiriers' rough-hewn kitchen table.

Poirier's wife was not well pleased. In all fairness, Joseph was simply following orders. William Hanington had sent word to move the body to a warm, well-lighted position so that it could be examined by the coroner, newly arrived from Dorchester.

The Poiriers' root cellar had been chosen to store its grim cargo by virtue of its proximity to the crime scene. In all of Shediac Parish, there was no hospital or doctor's surgery, no morgue or funeral home in which to store the victim. On February 14, as Mercy was pulled from the snow-bank near her brother's cabin, Poirier had agreed to store her body in his cellar while they awaited an inquest. Little did he realize Mercy's remains would take up residence in his house for the next six days.

Mercy's body, still locked in the fetal position in which she was found, had not weathered those days well. As a body thaws, signs of decomposition quickly set in. Her skin had turned from ghastly grey to a sickly mottled green. Her face was obscured by her hair, matted in blood. More blood and a rust-coloured fluid leaked from her wounds and natural orifices. As she thawed, the foul-smelling fluids seeped into the table and dripped onto the untreated floorboards. All the Poiriers could do was mask their faces against the noxious fumes and pray for the speedy arrival of Hanington and the coroner.

They were in for a long and miserable wait. The coroner for Westmorland County was not a man to be rushed. The office was held by Captain Gideon Palmer, an imposing figure of considerable reputation and influence. Educated, yet with an unmistakable rough-and-tumble air, the captain held himself in high regard but rarely extended the privilege to others. He moved through life at his own pace, which at the moment was maddeningly slow by the Poiriers' clock.

A consummate drinker, Palmer's face bore the ravages of a life of excess, aging him far beyond his fifty-five years. Born on October 29, 1749, in Westchester County, New York, to Philip Palmer and Sarah Hunt, Gideon had a secure, privileged upbringing but an errant heart.[2] At age twenty-seven, in the midst of the Revolutionary War, Gideon signed on with the British on Long Island and served as a lieutenant with the Westchester Refugees. It was his first glimpse of violent death, a sobering sight he revisited throughout his adult life.

During the conflict, Palmer enjoyed his fair share of scrapes with the law. He was once fined sixpence for breaking dishes during an altercation with Captain Henry Chapman in the mess at the general muster on Dixon's Island. At the close of the evening meal, for reasons known only to the two men, Chapman called Palmer out, exclaiming "you're a liar."[3] Palmer railed at the slight, jumping onto the table as he drew back to strike Chapman, inadvertently sending the table's contents crashing to the floor. Chapman emerged the victor of the altercation, and Palmer handed over his pay packet to replace the broken crockery. Perhaps the memory of that fine affords some explanation as to why Palmer seemed so fixated on the sum of sixpence, as will soon be evident.

After the war, Palmer tried his hand at business, partnering with a man named Titus Knapp at Fort Cumberland, Nova Scotia, but commerce bored him senseless. Gideon sold his share in the concern when he drew land in the lottery and moved west to Dorchester.[4] There, he joined the ranks of the Westmorland militia as a captain and married a local girl, Catharine Harper, the daughter of Christopher and Elizabeth Harper. Catharine was eighteen years his junior and quickly bore him nine children: four sons and five daughters.

A war wound had left Palmer with a slight limp, which grew more pronounced when he was fatigued or had imbibed heavily. The cannon had also left him hard of hearing, forcing others to shout to be heard. Palmer's infirmities, however, were not the cause of the six-day delay in investigating Mercy's death. Rather, the impediment stemmed from Palmer's political aspirations. Palmer punctuated his journey from Dorchester to Shediac with a series of stops at the homes of his cronies and political allies. The inquest into the death of Mercy Hall was to be his first homicide investigation as the king's coroner for Westmorland County, and Gideon Palmer wanted that fact to be well known.

With his glad-handing completed, Palmer at last set foot in Shediac Cape and got down to the brutal business at hand. He began his inquest by interviewing the relevant locals.[5] His first port of call was the home of William Hanington. After all, it was Hanington's letters to the justices of Westmorland that had alerted officials to the murder. The men settled into the sitting room with an ample supply of brandy and discussed the tragic events as gentlemen do. Hanington went on at length, acquainting the captain of the latest developments. With the liquor exhausted and daylight fading, the pair then set out to interview the other witnesses. As Hanington called out directions, the coroner's carriage sped through the tiny hamlet, stopping at the home of every English-speaking settler, where Palmer took the sworn oaths and witness statements of yeomen such as Samuel Cornwall, John Welling, and Amasa Killam, the men who had participated in the search for Mercy's remains. As he drew each interview to a close, Palmer instructed the man to head to the home of Joseph Poirier. Palmer needed a jury to witness his examination of the body, and since these men had already seen the victim at her worst, the coroner had little fear that an emotional outburst or fainting spell would call a halt to the grisly proceedings.

The inquest then continued with a cursory visit to the scene of the crime. Palmer and Hanington trudged through the snow toward the Babcocks' log cabin. Amos's wife Dorcas and the children stood sombrely as Palmer surveyed the room. The coroner noted the blood stains, still etched on the floorboards despite Dorcas's diligent cleaning efforts. Palmer also made his way to the snowbank where the body had been discovered, estimating the distance between the makeshift grave and the front door.

Returning to the cabin's tortured confines, Palmer then took a protracted statement from Dorcas, a crucial, though potentially biased, witness to the crime.[6] As she was illiterate, Palmer drafted her statement for her. During Dorcas's interview, Jonathon Babcock arrived at the cabin, answering a summons from Hanington to appear before the coroner. After finishing with Dorcas, Palmer turned his attention to Jonathon, faithfully committing the witness's words to paper, a harrowing account of impressive length and horrifying detail.

Before leaving the murder scene, Palmer had one last distasteful task to perform. In accordance with his duties as coroner — chief among them to protect the Crown's financial interests following an individual's death — Palmer had to prepare an inventory of Amos Babcock's personal estate. Although Amos had not yet been convicted of the crime, Palmer suspected the trial would not end in Babcock's favour. The law mandated that once Amos was formally tried and convicted, his estate must be sold off and the proceeds put into the king's coffers to cover the costs of his incarceration, prosecution, and eventual execution. Although propriety dictated Palmer wait until Babcock was executed, the coroner hoped to save himself another arduous journey north to Shediac.

In full view of Babcock's wife, brother, and children, Palmer took stock of the family's worldly goods, drafting an itemized list. It was a depressingly meagre collection, including three beds of varying types, two spinning wheels, five chairs, and some fishing equipment. The Crown was also entitled to any livestock and farming implements. Babcock's scant holdings included one cow, six pigs, and nine poultry, along with twenty-five bushels of wheat and a plough.[7] The coroner reckoned that Amos Babcock's earthly fortune amounted to a mere £18 5s. Palmer's hand-tailored coat likely cost more.

Palmer's ruthless task brought the harsh reality of the situation into sharp relief. Dorcas Babcock was about to lose what little she had left to her name. William Hanington, who counted himself among the family's friends and supporters, empathized with her humiliation and pain. Gideon Palmer, to the contrary, did not. With a perfunctory tip of his hat, he was off — the time had come to examine the victim's remains. Unlike their neighbours, neither Jonathon nor Dorcas Babcock was invited to attend the autopsy.

As Hanington and Palmer swept through their front door, the Poiriers were relieved to finally receive the coroner. The feeling was not mutual. Palmer did not speak French and had little time for the Acadians of Shediac. Despite being in the man's home, Palmer chose not to interview Joseph Poirier, nor did he speak to his sons, who had played such pivotal roles in Babcock's capture and arrest. Palmer's prejudicial view of the French was typical of the time. To the English, Acadians were distinct, almost a separate species. Even in Palmer's official correspondence, Acadians are referred to only as "the Frenchmen,"[8] unworthy to be called by their surnames.

Palmer also had no qualms in commandeering the Poiriers' modest farmhouse, now an ersatz morgue filled to capacity with the twelve local English-speaking yeomen — including Amasa Killam and Samuel Cornwall — whom Palmer had summoned to serve as the coroner's jury.[9] Custom and courtesy held that Mrs. Poirier offer hospitality to her uninvited guests, and the lady of the house was run ragged catering to the growing mob. At Palmer's urging, William Hanington agreed to serve as jury foreman. With that, the jurors were marshalled into the kitchen, where Mercy's decaying corpse lay in wait.

Although Gideon Palmer had some formal education, he was not a doctor nor did he possess any medical training. His duties as coroner required no such qualifications. In 1805 coroners were tax collectors, not medico-legal death investigators. Palmer needed only to confirm that Mercy Hall was, in fact, deceased and that she had died at the hand of another, thereby obligating said other to make reparations to the king. That said, it is clear from Palmer's report that he relished the opportunity to conduct his own particular brand of post-mortem examination and savoured the inherent shock value of an autopsy before a crowd of the uninitiated.

Surrounded by just such a crowd, the formal coroner's inquest began in the early evening of February 20, 1805. To open the proceedings, Palmer identified himself to the jurors as "a gentleman, one of the coroners of our Lord,"and attested to having seen the body of "Masala Hall there and then lying dead."[10] The jury concurred, no one troubling to correct Palmer regarding Mercy's given name.

Palmer then called the jury's attention to the murder weapon, which Hanington had held safe since the night of the crime. In his February 14 letter to Justice William Black, Hanington offered the following postscript: "I have the knife that he perpetrated the horrid deed with, it is still bloody."[11] Palmer failed to note the presence of blood in his official report, either because the blade had since been cleaned or because he did not find the presence of blood of any financial value to the Crown. Palmer detailed only two features of the blade: its length, which he recorded as seven inches, and its value, "a certain knife of the value of six pence."[12]

Turning now to the mortal remains of Mercy Hall, Palmer could not resist playing detective.[13] He deduced that Babcock had struck the fatal blows with his right hand, a conclusion that drew appreciative murmurs from the suitably awed jurors. Despite its tenure on the Poiriers' dining table, Mercy's body remained ice cold to the touch and could be made to lay flat only by force. As Palmer pushed apart Mercy's head and knees to examine her injuries, a vile cracking sound echoed off the cabin's log walls.

Wielding a candle and a kitchen knife to gain a better view of the injuries, Palmer informed his jury that he had identified the first blow: a wound to the centre of the breast, opening a gash two inches in breadth and six inches in depth. According to Palmer, the second blow fell to the

back of the head, tearing asunder the poor wench's scalp with a wound three inches long and half an inch deep. The coroner then declared that the *coup du grâce* had been struck to the stomach on the right side between the long ribs and the short ribs. This gash measured six inches in length and five inches in depth and had resulted in the partial disembowelment of Mercy's abdominal cavity.

Identifying the sequence of blows was little more than showboating on Palmer's part. There was no scientifically valid method of determining which blow came first, particularly given the coroner's absence of training and the embryonic state of forensic science at the time. Palmer's insights were not the product of expertise; he was a lay coroner conducting his first homicide investigation. Rather, they were simply lifted from the description of the killing contained in Dorcas Babcock's witness statement.

Having exhausted his sleights of hand, Gideon Palmer resumed his scrutiny of Mercy's traumatic injuries. As Palmer examined her head for further defects, clumps of her hair sloughed off in his hand, an artifact of her advanced stage of decay. Satisfied he had gained all he could from the body, Palmer gavelled the inquest to a close. After affixing their signatures to the report, the men of the coroner's jury were thanked for their service and summarily dismissed. When queried, Palmer declared that Mercy's body was to be returned to the family for burial.

Palmer then sat himself down in the homeowner's finest chair to complete his report for the court. An offer of whiskey was made and accepted. Palmer had no trouble accepting Poirier's hospitality, if not his word regarding the murder. Palmer never hedged from mixing business with pleasure, but he remained, first and foremost, a political operative. Scattered among the graphic details of Mercy's fatal injuries, Palmer inserted friendly greetings to the justices, passing on well wishes from their mutual acquaintances and family members in Shediac.

Ever mindful of the bottom line, Palmer ended his report with the following entreaty:

> If you proffer, I'd be obligated to you to mention to the
> Justices of Westmorland to have him [Amos Babcock] tried

as soon as possible as it will be saving a great expense to the county. I have the pleasure of saying the [illegible] family is all well and so is Mr. Wilson's and Mr. Knapps'.

Your humble servant
Gideon Palmer.[14]

His duties faithfully discharged, Palmer took his leave of the Poiriers, returning to the well-appointed rooms of Hanington's home for a nightcap and a recap of the day's events. The coroner had completed his first homicide investigation in record time. It would not be his last. Three years later, another murder rocked the county when Chandler Copp killed Park Davison.[15] Palmer would again be pressed into service to view the body and mind the Crown's financial interests in the untimely demise.

Speaking of money, Gideon Palmer ensured he was well compensated, and repeatedly so, for his sins in the case of Mercy Hall. Between June 12, 1806, and June 10, 1807, Palmer submitted no fewer than six separate invoices for his "expenses" in the Babcock investigation.[16] He received a total of £28 4s 7p, a very handsome sum for the time — a full £10 more than the estimated value of Babcock's entire estate.

The Long Ride Home

Late that evening, after Palmer took his victory lap and final curtain call, Jonathon Babcock made the sorrowful journey to the Poiriers' farm to claim his sister's remains. Joseph Poirier offered the use of his sleigh to transport the body, which Jonathon gratefully accepted. Poirier's sons gently placed Mercy on the sledge, the same carriage used to transport her killer only a week prior. The men helped Jonathon pull it to his house, where they transferred the body to the barn, offered their condolences, and dragged the sleigh back to their father's house.

Jonathon crafted a simple coffin out of spare wood. If any services were said, they were private. There was no memorial, no mass, no funeral procession. If anyone tried to contact Abner Hall to inform him of his wife's demise, no record of it survives. How or when Mercy's children heard of their mother's murder is also lost to the vicissitudes of time.

William Reynolds and his fellow chroniclers make no mention of what became of Mercy's remains. Our penchant for canonizing innocent murder victims is of relatively recent invention. In truth, once her body hit the floor, she ceased to be of interest to those purporting to tell the tragic tale of her murder. A voiceless bit player, having dutifully filled the role of victim, Mercy no longer served any narrative purpose, and what became of her seemed of little consequence. Amos Babcock and Jacob Peck were now the focus of the story.

It is said Mercy's body was laid to rest in a field not far from where Jonathon's house once stood on the road to Cocagne.[1] No marker stands to indicate the exact spot. Her sad life and violent death were venerated only in the memory of those who knew her story. Her final chapter was overlooked by those who claimed to tell it. She was poor, unwanted by her husband, and thought mad by the few in the village who knew her. Mercy Hall was a woman of no status or importance, her place in history secured only by the way she met her tragic end, and even then, only in the briefest of mentions.

The Accusation

William Hanington clearly had something on his mind. As he led coroner Gideon Palmer back to his home by the shores of Shediac Cape, Hanington saw his opportunity to unburden himself, and he seized it. The two men settled in the study, drinks in hand. William's wife, Mary, was as always a charming hostess but her husband quickly telegraphed his desire that she make herself scarce. At last at liberty to speak freely, Hanington told his distinguished and powerful guest of another dark misdeed that had taken place in Shediac of late — namely, the unseemly behaviour of Jacob Peck.

Palmer had heard the preacher's name bandied about earlier in the day. There was much talk of the revivals and Amos Babcock's growing religious fanaticism. But what Hanington told him now was something else entirely. William Hanington showed the coroner his transcription of Peck's last revival, the debacle on February 12 that led to Babcock's irrational act. To Hanington's way of thinking, Peck was as culpable for Mercy's death as Amos, a sentiment Hanington had freely shared with the preacher himself. He also regaled Palmer at length about Peck's prior religious services and the sweeping havoc wreaked on the small community since the evangelist had arrived.

Gideon Palmer paused to consider Hanington's concerns. Peck had quietly fled the village the day after the murder, leaving Palmer no chance to interview him directly. Palmer's role as coroner gave him broad scope and a rather amorphous authority in criminal matters. His mandate was to represent the Crown's financial interests and Palmer liked nothing better than to flex his judicial muscle, mandate be damned. As the evening progressed and the bottle grew lighter, Palmer came to share Hanington's conviction that Peck was guilty of some impropriety, even if the exact nature of his crime eluded them both at the moment.

After much reflection, Palmer instructed Hanington to write a letter to Westmorland Associate Justice Amos Botsford, cataloguing Jacob Peck's offences. For his part, Palmer would see to it that the matter was then presented to the grand jury for possible indictment. They would leave it to the judges and lawyers to decide exactly what law Peck had violated. This was, in Palmer's considered opinion, the best course of action, given that Peck was no longer in the district.

Overjoyed that his misgivings about Peck had fallen on such fertile ground, Hanington promised to draft the letter immediately.[1] He also felt certain he could convince others in the village who had witnessed Peck's unconventional sermons to offer similar evidentiary statements. Palmer concurred, drained his glass, and bid farewell to William and Mary Hanington.

Having satisfied his mandate regarding all manners of depravity in Shediac Parish, Palmer mounted his carriage and returned to his home in Dorchester. He submitted his inquest findings to the Westmorland justices of the peace,[2] accompanied by the various witness statements he had accrued. Discharging his service in the case of *The Crown v. Amos Babcock,* Palmer then made good on his promise to Hanington, bringing the matter of Jacob Peck to the court's attention. The local magistrates were intrigued and promised to review the case when Hanington's statement arrived.

Considering the matters of Babcock and Peck resolved to his satisfaction, Palmer took a moment to tell his wife of his travels and travails. He also relayed the greetings of their many acquaintances he had found time to visit en route.

Act 5   **The Preamble**

The murder of Mercy Hall had served Palmer well. His star was on the rise, and he had already prepared the necessary invoices to ensure he would be handsomely rewarded for his efforts. All in all, it was an impressive first effort for the county's novice homicide investigator, even if he alone voiced that opinion.

Irascible to the bitter end, Gideon Palmer died on October 6, 1824, in Saint John, just days shy of his seventy-fifth birthday. According to his obituary, "his dust reposes at the Dorchester Cemetery,"[3] next to that of his wife, who outlived him by eight years.

William Hanington also made good on his word. Even as Palmer's carriage cut fresh tracks in the snow outside his home, William was at his desk, quill in hand, committing to paper each of Peck's affronts to common decency. In what fast became a comprehensive screed, Hanington recorded the infernal cleric's every word and action since the man first set foot in the village. Writing through the night, Hanington even documented his own exhaustion and haste, closing his missive: "I have related the heads of things in a great hurry, as I thought it my duty to both to [sic] King & Country to make it known. You will meet with many improprieties & bad writing, which I hope you will excuse, as I have been writing [a] great part of the night & am now writing with out any fire as my house is full of people."[4]

Hanington's sense of urgency was infectious, if not entirely necessary. He included the postscript: "PS — the gentlemen of the Jury are now waiting for this letter,"[5] lest the Westmorland magistrates fail to recognize the imperative nature of his deposition. Hanington dated his letter February 21, 1805, and addressed it to Amos Botsford, Associate Justice of Westmorland County. Having done his duty "to King & Country," Hanington left his house full of people[6] without fire and staggered off to bed.

A Lesser Evil

[1]

[2]

The Hanington letter...was intended to initiate
Peck's prosecution, although the writer did not
quite know for what.
— David Graham Bell, 1984[3]

Suffice it to say that determining what law Jacob Peck had violated with his mongrel revivals landed well outside the very limited scope of William Hanington's civic duties. That task fell to two key figures in the next act of the continuing saga of Amos Babcock and Jacob Peck. They were the Botsfords, Amos and William, an upstanding educated father and son duo with a long and fabled history. Yet for all their lofty status and storied learning, the Botsfords — particularly Botsford Jr. — were responsible for the most egregious blunder in what was rapidly becoming a judicial comedy of errors.

The elder Botsford, Amos, was born in Newtown, Connecticut, on January 30, 1744.[4] Grown into manhood, he was an ardent Loyalist, and when such affiliations no longer proved popular in Connecticut, he sailed north with his young son William and wife Sarah to Annapolis Royal, Nova Scotia. Amos's eventual rise to glory stemmed from humble roots. In his newly adopted country, he held a series of relatively low-level governmental posts. By 1778 he had scraped together enough money to buy a large parcel of land near Westcock, in what would soon be neighbouring New Brunswick. There, Amos Botsford was determined to build his family's reputation and fortune.

As the years passed, Amos's status grew to match his ambitions. Yeoman Botsford eventually became the Honourable Amos Botsford, Esquire, Barrister at Law. Amos then branched into politics, adding to his swelling resumé by becoming speaker of the House of Assembly. In 1784 Amos was elected Representative of Westmorland, an office he held until his death at age sixty-nine.

Amos demanded excellence of himself and accepted no less from his only son. He sent the boy to Yale University, where William earned top marks. When William graduated in 1792 at the tender age of nineteen, Amos summoned his son back to New Brunswick, where Amos had secured a place for him under the tutelage of the Honourable Jonathon Bliss, then Attorney General and later chief justice of the Supreme Court. After studying at the feet of Judge Bliss, William passed the bar and began his own modest legal practice. To his father's delight, William also married well, claiming the hand of Sarah Lowell, a woman of remarkable beauty and impressive pedigree.

By February 1805, the Honourable Amos Botsford had risen to the rank of justice of the peace for Westmorland, one of several such magistrates for the county. Botsford was chosen to oversee the grand jury sessions of Shediac troublemakers Amos Babcock and Jacob Peck. Suitably honoured by the commission, Amos Botsford's first order of business was to appoint his son William as chief prosecutor, tasked with arguing the felony cases before the panel. It was, in hindsight, a catastrophic error. With this overt act of nepotism, Botsford Sr. had sidestepped countless far more experienced and qualified candidates.

The resulting hue and cry from aggrieved lawyers mattered little to Amos Botsford. He knew the precedent-setting cases, and his son's central role in them, would propel William into the lofty social stratosphere he himself currently occupied. History proved him right. Upon Amos Botsford's death — which occurred in the early morning hours of Tuesday, September 15, 1812, in Saint John — son William succeeded his father as Representative of Westmorland. Following literally in his father's sizable footsteps, William got himself elected to his father's former post as speaker of the Assembly. Eventually, William stepped out of his father's shadow, donning a robe Amos had only dreamed of. In 1824 William Botsford was appointed to the Supreme Court of New Brunswick. William served the court faithfully for twenty years, retiring in 1844 only when his progressive deafness forced him to step down. William enjoyed another twenty years of retirement, succumbing at the ripe old age of ninety-two.

The innate Botsford drive to succeed passed to the next generation. William Botsford was survived by six overachieving sons who dedicated their lives to the service of their county: William Jr., a doctor; Amos, a senator; Bliss, a judge; Chipman, a Representative in the Assembly; George, who was clerk of the Legislative Council; and Blair, who served as both sheriff of Westmorland County and warden of the Dorchester Penitentiary.

Yet for all the Botsfords' laudable exploits, it was the trial of an illiterate yeoman, charged with the brutal slaying of his sister in an apparent fit of religious fervour, and the bewildering case of a wayward preacher who may or may not have violated some yet-to-be-determined law that ultimately would secure their places in infamy. In the spring of 1805, Amos Botsford was an elder statesman and jurist, in the twilight of a towering career. He was sixty-one years of age. William had just turned thirty-three.

The trial of Amos Babcock would be the first homicide case for either Botsford. In 1805 the legal system in New Brunswick was still in its infancy and experiencing considerable growing pains. British common law was the de facto rule of the land, but enforcement had more to do with luck, geography, and the social status of the accused. The fault did not rest in any one sphere. Judges were trained but hamstrung by a penal code not yet written or ratified. Sheriffs and constables had little actual authority and were burdened with multicultural jurisdictions and enormous territories to police. Jails were few, far between, and woefully ill-equipped.

Into this chaotic fray stepped young William Botsford, blindingly ambitious, more than a little arrogant and entitled, and — in his quest to impress his father — not the least inclined to admit his shortcomings or ask for assistance.

In all fairness to William, no one in the provincial legal system had much experience when it came to murder trials. The Crown's case against Amos Babcock was only the third murder trial in New Brunswick's short history. The first actual homicide ever tried in the province was never included in the official tally because both the victim and accused were black — and therefore not recognized as "people" under the law — and because the verdict had been reduced to manslaughter.[5] The second murder trial — and first official homicide on the provincial tally — exposed the deeply entrenched racial divide separating European settlers from the Aboriginals whose land they had colonized.

That murder occurred on May 20, 1786. Two Queen's Rangers — David Nelson and his commander, William Harboard — had gone fishing just before dawn.[6] The two men heard dogs barking at Nelson's house and returned to find two strays eating one of his hogs. Harboard shot the dogs while Nelson went to check on the livestock in his barn. Nelson found all his hogs stolen and surmised the thieves must have loaded the swine into a boat. The men searched the river, soon coming upon a group of Maliseet hunters a quarter-mile upstream. The Rangers ordered the hunters to stop and accused them of stealing the hogs. The Maliseet in turn accused the Rangers of shooting their dogs and proceeded to paddle away.

Harboard suggested firing a warning shot over their heads to halt their retreat. The two men fired several shots, stopping to reload their weapons after each round. The Rangers claimed they fired with no intent to kill or wound, seeking only to frighten the hunters into returning the hogs. When the gunsmoke cleared, Harboard and Nelson saw a lone canoe in the river. As they approached the boat, they found Pierre Benoit, one of the Aboriginal hunters, dead in the canoe. The Rangers were later arrested and charged with murder.[7]

The First Nations community, accustomed to receiving inequitable justice at the hands of European settlers, demanded an immediate decision

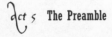

regarding the fate of the Rangers. The trial was held less than a month later, the first in the newly completed courthouse in the provincial capital, Fredericton. Supreme Court Chief Justice George Duncan Ludlow and Justice Isaac Allen presided. Ward Chipman served as chief prosecutor.

The trial ignited a firestorm of controversy and outrage. What, if any, punishment two white men accused of killing an Aboriginal should face sparked heated debate and exposed thinly veiled bigotry on both sides.[8] Typical of the racist rhetoric was this statement by prosecution witness Edward Winslow, who wrote that he feared "two men of fair character should be sacrificed to satisfy the barbarous claims of a set of savages."[9]

The prisoners were not defended by counsel, standard practice of the day even for those charged with capital offences. The prosecution called three witnesses, including the savage-baiting Edward Winslow, but no one from the First Nation band who had witnessed the attack. There was no need; the jury quickly delivered the verdict: guilty. The two men were sentenced to hang on June 23, 1786, nine days after the trial.

First Nations leaders were satisfied with the verdict; the English settlers were not. To curtail rioting, the court adopted a risky, almost schizophrenic plan. To appease the Aboriginals, David Nelson — who had fired the fatal shot — was hanged as scheduled. Days later, William Harboard was quietly pardoned when fears of an Aboriginal uprising were quelled by Nelson's execution. Such was the capricious nature of frontier justice in the decades before Canada declared itself a sovereign nation.

The race to justice evident in the Nelson/Harboard trial raised serious questions regarding the province's system of jurisprudence, particularly as it related to murder and the executions such crimes engendered. Some twenty years later, the Supreme Court was determined to learn from past mistakes, and the case of *The King v. Amos Babcock* was to be a showcase, a true master class in how to try a capital murder case. It was a noble, if somewhat unrealistic, goal.

Quixotically pursing this impossible dream, Amos Botsford assembled the evidence gathered to date and presented it to his son. For a homicide investigation, the documentation was disturbingly scant. Undaunted, father and son — pathologically competitive and unaccustomed to failure — viewed the murder of Mercy Hall as an open-and-shut case. The crime had been heinous, but as a matter of law, the case was straightforward and undemanding. No fewer than twelve people, albeit many of them children, had witnessed the actual crime, and the accused never denied his actions — only his guilt in the eyes of God. In the minds of the Botsfords, the conviction of the defendant was inevitable, almost a foregone conclusion. As for Peck — whose indiscretions would also be presented to the same grand jury — his case was given short shrift. The preacher's actions paled in comparison to the murderous act of Babcock, and the question remained: what, if any, crime had he committed?

For all his Byzantine machinations, Jacob Peck did not evade criminal responsibility for the totality of his crimes through his own cunning or wiles. As fate would have it, he escaped justice because of the relative youth, inexperience, and ambition of William Botsford.

True Bills

Peck's and Babcock's march toward justice began as William Botsford empanelled his grand jury. Twenty-four men of Westmorland County — chosen for their sobriety, integrity, and forthright characters — were assembled at the Dorchester Courthouse on February 22, 1805. The pro forma jury foreman was the clerk of the court, Hezekiah King, tasked with recording the outcome of the proceedings. Also on the panel was Christopher Horsman,[1] fated to become Jacob Peck's brother-in-law in one year's time. The English-speaking community of the county was a very small world indeed.

Justice Amos Botsford gavelled the proceedings to order. The men were duly sworn and seated. Jurors were warned that grand jury testimony was sealed; they were not to repeat anything they heard outside the courthouse. This no doubt came as a disappointment to some, who saw their summons as a licence to drink from the fountainhead of village gossip.

William Botsford stepped forward and introduced himself. Scanning the men before him, he found himself at an immediate disadvantage. He was years, in some cases decades, younger than the jurors whose respect and trust he desperately needed in order to be effective. To certify himself as a legal expert, Botsford began with a civics lesson. He offered a lengthy introduction to the process, informing the jurors what they might expect and what was expected of them. Having established his credentials, and much to the jury's relief, William Botsford at last segued into their raison d'être: the Crown's case against Amos Babcock. The time had come for Botsford Jr. to present the evidence to the panel.

Unlike a typical trial, members of the grand jury would not hear directly from witnesses; rather, their sworn statements were read aloud to the court.[2] William Botsford opened with his most shocking evidence: the coroner's report outlining Mercy's appalling injuries in graphic, bloody detail. In the days before crime-scene photos, the coroner's report was the closest any jurors came to experiencing the full horror of the act for themselves.

One by one, Botsford then read aloud the statements of Jonathon Babcock, Dorcas Babcock, William Hanington, Amasa Killam, and Samuel Cornwall.[3] Although many of the affidavits recounted the same events over and over, each contributed some unique and critical piece of the puzzle. Botsford's aim was to give the jurors as comprehensive a picture of the crime as possible. Brevity was sacrificed on the altar of scrupulous detail. Further, no physical evidence — including the murder weapon — was presented to the jury; words alone had to suffice, and William Botsford fed the jury every word at his disposal.

As was standard with grand jury hearings, no one spoke for the defence, and the panel was given no opportunity to discuss the case or debate the evidence. When he had at last exhausted his arsenal of witness accounts, Botsford asked the jury to vote on a true bill against Amos Babcock. A yes vote meant Babcock would be indicted and tried for the crime. A nay vote would signal that the jury believed there was insufficient evidence to press charges.

Botsford's verbosity notwithstanding, the case against Babcock was strong. Whatever his motivation — the as-yet unnamed tempest that had raged in Amos's head — Babcock had held the knife that had slain his sister. With one voice, the men of the grand jury voted for the true bill, empowering the justices of Westmorland to indict Amos Babcock. As Babcock was already in custody, separated from the jury only by the tavern beneath their feet, no arrest warrant was necessary. Because of the heinous nature of the crime, release on bail was not an option.

With Babcock suitably dispatched, Botsford then turned the jury's

 Act 5 **The Preamble**

attention to the matter of Jacob Peck. It was a moment Botsford had secretly dreaded. The case against Peck was weak to the point of collapsing, a chimera of innuendo, accusation, and moral outrage against which Botsford could find no suitable legal weapon. The good citizens of Shediac Parish were united in their belief that Peck was guilty of something, but what? Clearly, the preacher had offended the villagers' sense of decorum, but that in itself did not constitute a criminal offence.

Botsford had given the matter some thought and had arrived at a safe, if somewhat unsatisfying, conclusion. Based on the witness statements, it was clear to Botsford that Peck's sermons represented acts of blasphemy and sedition. The evangelist had proclaimed himself to be John the Baptist, a sacrilegious defilement. Furthermore, Peck professed on at least two occasions to be in direct contact with that other most sovereign Lord, King George III. Peck had wantonly declared in public that the monarchy would not survive another ten years, an overt act of treason committed with profane and seditious language. The indictment stopped well short of murder, but the young prosecutor felt certain he could prove the lesser charges with the evidence he had on hand.

Accordingly, after a brief presentation, William Botsford charged the men of the jury to vote a true bill against Peck on the sole charge of using seditious and blasphemous language. Having heard the depositions of Hanington and others, the panel's decision was swift and sure: the grand jury voted unanimously to indict Jacob Peck for blasphemy and sedition. Under Britain's notorious "Bloody Code,"[4] such offences were met with the hangman's noose, but in the colonies struggling to free themselves from such draconian rule, Peck's punishment was far less certain.

Although the indictment undoubtedly proved disappointing to William Hanington, who believed the invidious Peck had had a hand in Mercy's demise, the question of the preacher's culpability in Hall's murder was never raised before the grand jury. The cases of Babcock and Peck were kept separate, and jurors had no latitude to consider indicting Peck for any other crime. That fateful decision rested solely on the novice head of William Botsford.

Grand juries are held in camera; no transcripts thus exist of William

Botsford's pleas to the panel. The jury members, forbidden to speak publicly regarding the evidence, remained true to their oath. An exhaustive search of the archives failed to unearth a single letter, journal entry, or indiscreet snippet by any of the jurors relating to what they heard or saw that day. The only documentation generated by the process was the true bills and indictments issued as a result, as well as some perfunctory notes in the minutes of the court. As such, William Botsford's reasoning was never recorded or made public.

Whatever his thinking, Botsford elected not to pursue Peck in the death of Mercy Hall. Based on the evidence, his decision defies conventional wisdom. Botsford Jr. certainly had the option to do so, courtesy of a very recent precedent that had been set as the result of a three-shilling theft. Less than four years prior, the trial of *The Crown v. Higgins* had defined an entirely new crime, that of solicitation or incitement. In 1801 Mr. Higgins had convinced a manservant, James Dixon, "to take, embezzle or steal a quantity of twist, of the value of three shillings" from his master,[5] Mr. J. Philips. Caught red-handed in the act, Dixon told authorities he had been enticed to commit the theft by Higgins. The court found the manservant guilty of theft but, more to the point, also charged Higgins with inciting the crime.

The landmark decision meant that anyone who advocated, promoted, or encouraged another to violate the law could themselves stand accused of incitement, regardless of whether the solicited crime was ever committed. Although the law had yet to be applied to capital crimes such as murder, there was no legal impediment to doing so.

Although the whys and wherefores are lost to history, William Botsford failed to charge Peck with inciting the murder. The blame rests with Botsford's unseasoned nature — either he was unaware of the new law or was reluctant to apply it in this case. Whether it was ignorance or fear that hobbled Botsford, the result was the same: Jacob Peck would not be held accountable in the death of Mercy Hall. For his sins, Peck would receive little more than a judicial slap on the wrist, thanks in no small part to William Botsford.

straw man A person hired to post a worthless bail bond to secure the release of the accused.

Guaranteed

Leonard Peck[1]

Armed with the grand jury's true bill, Justice William Black wasted no time issuing an arrest warrant for Jacob Peck. The writ contained express orders "commanding the Constables of Dorchester to apprehend Jacob Peck of Petitcodiac."[2] The Constables of Dorchester — Lockwood Baxter, Asa Fillmore, James Harrcott, Gideon Smith, and Samuel Bishop, led by High Constable Ralph Siddall — proved unequal to the task.[3] Peck was not apprehended, although in deference to the constables, the preacher was nowhere near Petitcodiac. He had returned to his home in Salisbury Parish, well outside their jurisdiction.

More paperwork was to follow. The next day, Justice Black issued a writ entitled *The King v. Jacob Peck*. The indictment formally charged Peck with using "blasphemous and seditious language,"[4] based on the sworn testimony of William Hanington, Amasa Killam, and Dorcas Babcock. The bill held no kind words for the accused: "Jacob Peck, late of the Parish of Dorchester, being a prophane, wicked and blasphemous man and a wicked and base imposter and sullier of the sacred Scriptures of the New Testament and contriving and intending to personate and to present himself to be John the Baptist mentioned in the holy gospels of God."[5]

As expected, the indictment failed to mention the death of Mercy Hall. Peck's crimes — having "derision and contempt for the Christian religion"and a patent disrespect for His Majesty[6] — were isolated to the revival of February 12. Jacob's insistence that Hanington record the prophesies of Babcock's teenage daughter had come back to haunt him.

The constables of Dorchester failed to apprehend Peck, but word of his arrest warrant reached him at his home in Salisbury. On February 25, 1805, Jacob Peck surrendered himself to the Dorchester Courthouse. He was there met by Robert Keillor, who temporarily abandoned his post as bar keep to fulfill his role as jail keep. Keillor summoned the clerk of the court, Hezekiah King, who in turned roused a local justice of the peace, the Honourable James Watson, Esquire. Watson quickly donned his wig and gown and brought the court into session.

The unrepentant cleric was brought before the bar and Watson read aloud his indictment. When asked, Peck entered his plea — a resounding not guilty. With that, the case was no longer in the hands of the Honourable Judge Watson. The charges against Peck were felonious and therefore exceeded the jurisdiction of the local Westmorland court, which normally concerned itself with civil issues of probate and chancery. The matter was remanded to the New Brunswick Supreme Court, to be heard at the next session of the circuit court. The courthouse would stay the same; only the bench need change.

The delay raised the question of what to do with Peck until his court date. Unlike Amos Babcock, currently mouldering in the dungeon two floors below, bail was an option for Jacob. Anticipating as much, the preacher had arrived prepared, coin at the ready.

Given the severity of the charges, and the nomadic nature of the accused, bail was set at the substantial sum of £400 sterling. Without batting an eye, Peck presented the court a £50 bond, which the judge accepted. In light of Peck's rather impoverished circumstance, the money likely came from his family, either Martin Sr. or Jr. Although £50 exceeded Peck's annual income, it was a small price to pay to maintain his freedom.

As was customary for yeomen and those unknown to the court, Peck was required to provide guarantors: upstanding citizens to vouch for Peck and assure the court of his eventual return to face trial. Such sureties were more than mere character witnesses; they had to put up their own money as a testament to their sincerity. Normally one drew guarantors from the more respected ranks of their acquaintances, but Peck had no such luxury. His choice of sureties was telling in that they were two men of lesser social prominence than the preacher himself: his younger brother Leonard and a man named Reuben Mills.[7]

Leonard Peck, nine years Jacob's junior, was a farmer and occasional constable for Westmorland. That Leonard vouchsafed Jacob's honour was a predictable, if somewhat foolhardy, act of sibling fealty. Less comprehensible was the willingness of Peck's other surety, Reuben Mills, to put his reputation, and money, on the line.

Scant trace remains of Reuben Mills today.[8] At the time, Mills was a resident of Dorchester. Like Jacob Peck, Mills had served as a constable, in his case in Moncton in 1790 and in Dorchester in 1804. He had also been a Fence-viewer on a number of occasions. His family had originated in Bedford, New York, likely carried north in the Loyalist wave at the end of the Revolutionary War. Shrugging off his humble roots, in 1789 Mills married Deborah Lewis of a well-heeled Loyalist family. The couple had eight children. Despite his in-laws' wealth and prestige, when Reuben Mills died seventeen years later in March 1822, he was a very poor man with limited worldly goods and no discernible social station.

Given Mills's strong Loyalist ties, he seems an odd choice to endorse a man accused of sedition. What, if any, acquaintance Jacob Peck and Reuben Mills had prior to their joint appearance in the courthouse that day has escaped notice in the historical record. Chances are Mills was simply a bondsman, paid by Peck for his services.

As sureties, both Leonard Peck and Reuben Mills were each required to pay an additional £25 bond, a strong incentive to ensure Jacob appeared in court as scheduled. With the bail secured, Judge Watson released Jacob Peck on his own recognizance, with the understanding that the full bond would be forfeited if Peck failed to meet the following conditions: "-1- that Jacob Peck shall personally appear at the next general session of the peace to be holden in and for the said county and -2- that he shall be of good behaviour towards the King."[9]

As Judge Watson's gavel sounded, Jacob Peck was once again a free man.

Material Witness

Jonathan Babcock[1]

As Peck held his ground in the dock of the Dorchester Courthouse, buying his freedom, the legal workings in the case against Amos Babcock continued apace. Based on the true bill handed down by the grand jury, the formal indictment was issued the next day.[2] Pulsating with vivid detail, *The King against Amos Babcock* summarized the findings of the coroner's inquest, recounting every wound inflicted on the body of Mercy Hall and offering salacious particulars of the night in question. These damning tidbits were drawn from the witness statements of Amasa Killam, Samuel Cornwall, and Lucy Bramble, as well as the depositions of William Hanington, Jonathon Babcock, and Amos's wife, Dorcas. The writ also noted a newcomer to the witness roster: jailer Robert Keillor, whose first-hand observations of Babcock in captivity would soon dispel any notion Amos was innocent by reason of insanity.

Crazy or not, Amos remained in custody at the Dorchester jail under Keillor's watchful eye. As Babcock was without the services of a defence attorney, court clerk Hezekiah King delivered the writ to Amos in his cell. Unable to read or write, Amos had no understanding of what he was handed. King likely took pity on the accused and read Amos the indictment, then returned the document to his office for safekeeping.

Amos was not the only Babcock garnering the court's attention. On March 6, 1805, Jonathon Babcock, already identified as a key witness for the prosecution, was called before the bar at the Dorchester Courthouse, even as his brother lay shackled in its jail. To ensure his continued co-operation with the prosecution's case against his kin, the justices of the peace of Westmorland County had issued a writ of bail for Jonathon Babcock in the staggering amount of £500 "lawful money."[3] The writ stated, "the nature of this obligation is such that the aforementioned Jonathon Babcock does and shall appear on behalf of our Sovereign Lord the King for the trial of Amasa Babcock (touching the death of Masala Hall)."[4] Court clerk Hezekiah King had taken the incorrect versions of Amos's and Mercy's names directly from the inquest report of Gideon Palmer and transposed them onto the indictment. As the trial progressed, King recognized his error and corrected it in subsequent court records.[5]

A struggling crofter, Jonathon had never seen £500 in his entire life, a fact the court used to its distinct advantage. Failure to pay the bond would result in Jonathon's incarceration, forcing him to share the same cell as his brother until the trial. Like Peck, Jonathon also required a number of sureties to swear to his good character and future compliance. Desperate to avoid the jail, Jonathon pleaded with his friends and neighbours to serve as guarantors, as well for any financial aid they might be willing to give. Intimately aware of his plight, Jonathon's saving grace came in the forms of William and Mary Hanington, Amasa Killam, and John Welling, themselves slated as witnesses in the upcoming trial. The four agreed to serve as sureties for Jonathon Babcock.[6] That pledge cost them £500.

The inclusion of Mary Hanington was unusual, as women then rarely served as sureties. Her willingness to vouch for Jonathon attested to his integrity; that the court accepted her as a guarantor spoke volumes about her impeccable reputation and standing in the community.

Another curious, gender-specific artifact of the times is that an equally crucial prosecution witness — Dorcas Babcock — was not similarly bonded. Sex aside, the different treatment of Dorcas and Jonathon stemmed from their respective relationships to the accused. The bias originated in common law, which held that a husband and wife be regarded as one person, with the husband deemed the head.[7] Since the law also prohibited self-incrimination, a wife could not be compelled to testify against her husband. Dorcas's decision to bear witness against Amos flew sharply in the face of social convention. That she elected to testify against her husband says a great deal about the seriousness of the crime, the state of their relationship, and Dorcas's strength of character.

With Jonathon's bail set, all was now ready. The matters of Amos Babcock and Jacob Peck were moved to the top of the docket for the next court session. The county prepared for the much-anticipated event with a bewildering mix of civic pride and collective shame. Robert Keillor supervised the final touches to the hastily constructed courthouse, jail, and tavern, a final burst of renovation to help accommodate the capacity crowds expected. With the paint not yet dry, the trials were to be the first held in the new Dorchester Courthouse, his brother John Keillor's master-stroke of political manoeuvring. It would also be the first murder case in the province tried outside Saint John, then the capital. Although it was the product of tragic circumstances, the district was eager and even a wee bit toffee-nosed to play host to such a momentous occasion.

The Botsfords wrapped up the last of their court-appointed tasks. A list of potential jurors was drawn up and all exhibits (including the physical evidence, scant though it might be) were organized. Despite the aggressive campaigning of his father, William Botsford was not chosen to lead the prosecution for the actual trials. With discernible regret, he stood ready to hand the case on to a far more seasoned prosecutor, downplaying the slight to all those who inquired.

With everything well in hand, all eyes turned to the road leading to Saint John as they awaited the arrival of the circuit court judge who would serve as ringmaster over the coming spectacle.

nisi prius [Latin, "unless before then"]
A system of judicial circuits in which judges
are assigned for local trials of civil and criminal
cases, to be presented before a jury.

Jurisprudent

[signature: J. Upham][1]

Judge Joshua Upham was in a particularly foul mood. The Honourable Mr. Upham, Puisne Justice of the Supreme Court of New Brunswick, was trapped in his own private hell, though one not entirely of his own making. For the moment, that hell was his personal carriage, making the bone-rattling journey from his home in French Village, just west of Fredericton, to the courthouse in Dorchester, some one hundred and fifty miles to the east. Recent rains had reduced what normally passed for roads to rutted, impassable swamps. His new driver seemed hell-bent on destroying the carriage and the judge along with it. Upham, who suffered from rheumatoid arthritis, felt every lurch in his eroded joints.[2]

The carriage itself did not help matters. It was fine enough, a little tired and worn perhaps, but Upham felt his exalted post warranted something a bit more genteel. He had seen much finer coaches throughout town, transporting men of far lesser import than himself. His carriage was symptomatic of the greater problem — namely, his salary. As a Supreme Court justice, albeit a junior one, Upham was entitled to a yearly stipend of £300 sterling, an outrageous pittance in his eyes.[3] Although his salary was more than some yeomen saw in a lifetime — including that wastrel Babcock, the source of the judge's current woes — Upham viewed it as a slap in the face, an insult to a man of his distinction, education, and expertise.

Upham was bred to expect more from life. Born in Brookfield, Massachusetts, in 1741, Joshua was the favoured son of Dr. Jabez Upham, who practised medicine just outside Boston.[4] Dr. Upham demanded the best education money could buy for his son. Joshua attended Harvard, graduating in 1763, although his degree had nothing to do with the law — Harvard would not open its school of law until 1817. Young Joshua was not brilliant but he was a hard worker, and Upham's modest academic success was the result of application rather than aptitude. Although he did not exceed his father's lofty expectations, Joshua managed neither to distinguish nor to embarrass himself.

With so much given, much was expected. The good doctor wanted his son to study medicine or law, and Joshua chose the latter. A career in jurisprudence suited Joshua's regimented nature and lust for argument. After graduation, Upham began a study of the law in Brookfield. He even married Mary, the daughter of a judge: the Honourable John Murray of Rutland, Massachusetts. The future magistrate's dreams were put on hold, however, with the start of the Revolutionary War. Upham sided with the Crown, fighting with the King's American Dragoons. By the end of the war, he had made colonel. Joshua Upham had proven his mettle in battle, was a Harvard-educated man from a moneyed family, but for the first time in his young life, he found himself on the wrong side of a fight. He, along with his fellow Loyalists, ventured northward.

The move was not entirely politically motivated. Following the Expulsion of the Acadians from New Brunswick, Governor Lawrence had issued a bold proclamation, offering free land and favourable terms to any English-speaking New Englander willing to settle in the northern territory. Upham drew a tract of land — some fourteen hundred acres — near French Village,[5] ideally situated between the burgeoning towns of Saint John and Fredericton, and resumed his career in politics and law. He was elected to a seat on the legislative council, and in shockingly short order, appointed a Supreme Court justice in 1786.

Upham had served the court faithfully for almost twenty years, yet an aged coach and a miserly wage was all he had to show for it. As his carriage rolled on, the judge, lost in his miseries, received a harsh wake-up call. While crossing a rickety bridge, the carriage spun out of control, endangering the lives of Upham, the driver, and the horse.[6] The mishap jolted Upham, sending him cursing against the roof of his carriage. After a quick repair to a wheel, the journey continued.

As he suffered his way through the final miles to Dorchester, Upham was in his sixty-fourth year, a time of life when men normally prepare to retire and live out their legacy. Upham had no such option. His contemptible salary was insufficient to keep him and his family in any decent manner and he had accrued no savings worth mentioning. Upham — battered, bruised, and forlorn — had little choice but to soldier on and work till he dropped.

As the carriage wheels fought for purchase in the mire, Upham sank deep into his seat. At moments such as these, the judge could not help but wonder if he was being punished for some past infraction. He could no longer deny that his recent ruling on the incendiary issue of slavery had left him ostracized and vilified, a pariah in the court.

The contentious case had come before the entire Supreme Court bench in 1800.[7] A black woman, Nancy Morton, was protesting her enslavement to Caleb Jones, a Loyalist. Jones claimed to have bought Nancy from another Loyalist — William Bailey of York County, New Brunswick — for the sum of £40. Jones was given title to the woman when the money changed hands. In response to her complaint, a fellow justice, Isaac Allen, issued a warrant instructing Jones to bring Morton to court and justify his "ownership" of her.

At the time, the four-man bench was made up of three slave owners — Chief Justice George Duncan Ludlow, Justice Allen, and Judge Upham — and John Saunders, the lone jurist with no slaves. Since its separation from Nova Scotia on August 16, 1784, New Brunswick had been without laws regarding slavery, and the Morton case ignited a racially charged debate that pitted slavers against abolitionists.

In a split decision that managed to anger both sides, Ludlow and Upham upheld the slave owner's rights, while Allen and Saunders sided with Morton. Chief Justice Ludlow cast the deciding vote, and Nancy was returned to Caleb Jones. Following the hearing, Judge Allen decided to set his own slaves free. Upham, with fourteen hundred free acres to cultivate, elected to keep his.

He now regretted the decision. In the years following the landmark ruling, the tide had turned against slavery in the fledgling province. Public sentiment now favoured the abolitionists and Upham once again found himself on the wrong side of a fight. Judge Upham also had a far more personal reason to regret his polemic pro-slavery stance. Among Upham's slave holdings were six individuals whom his wife, Mary, had inherited from her father. One of those slaves, Luke Hamilton, had once been Upham's most trusted servant. Luke frequently had accompanied Upham on the circuit, serving as his driver and valet. Yet the judge's trust had been misplaced. On one occasion, Luke told a white man in passing, "if he thought Master would sell him, he would kill him."[8]

Luke never made good on the threat as far as the judge was concerned, but in 1802 — less than two years after Upham had upheld his own right to keep slaves — Luke Hamilton killed a girl named Alice West.[9] At the time of the offence, Luke was just twenty-three, a muscular, imposing man. Upham had sent him to the city on horseback to conduct some business. On his return trip, Luke travelled along the old Westmorland Road. The girl was on the same road, picking berries. When she did not return home that afternoon, a search was mounted and her body later found. She had been stabbed repeatedly and sexually assaulted.

Suspicion quickly fell on Luke, who denied having anything to do with the crime. Skilled at interrogation, Upham fired a series of innocuous questions at Luke, then quickly asked him what he had done with the knife. Without thinking, Luke replied: "hid it under a stump, Massa." The weapon was soon found, as were hoofprints from Luke's horse near the spot where the girl's body had been dumped. Luke was brought to Saint John and, in due course, tried and convicted. In the hours before his execution, Luke offered a full confession.

Joshua Upham's learned opinion on the matter of slavery now left him in an untenable position. His ruling, defining slaves as property rather than as people, placed Upham at the centre of an imponderable ethical dilemma: was Upham, as Luke's owner, now legally culpable for

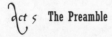

the rape and murder of the girl, violations that had been caused by his property? Were it not so personal, it would have been a fascinating legal question. Had Upham's horse run amok and destroyed the chattels of another, he would have been held responsible for damages; was the same not true of the actions of Luke? Fortunately for Upham (and Upham alone), the question was rendered moot because of Alice West. The victim was herself a black slave and therefore also not a "person," making Luke's offence a civil property matter rather than one of criminal concern. Litigations involving Blacks were not considered legitimate cases under New Brunswick law. Although Hamilton's trial preceded Babcock's by three years, Luke never appeared in the official tally that counted Amos Babcock as only the second "person" to be tried for murder in the province.

Thanks to Upham and Ludlow, slavery was not illegal in New Brunswick but the practice had come to be viewed as morally repugnant. In the wake of the Supreme Court ruling, the newspaper editorials had been scathing. One community on the Bay of Fundy went so far as to post signs on its borders reading "no slave masters admitted."[10] As he sat in his carriage, en route to Dorchester, Upham was still a slave owner in a province that no longer condoned the trade, a precarious position to hold. Despite the court's decision, the abolitionist movement gained momentum, and by 1822 no slaves would remain in New Brunswick, although official emancipation would not come until 1836.

Perhaps Upham thought his banishment to the rural circuit was retribution for his reviled stance on slavery, condemning him eternally to wander the back roads of every paltry village in this godforsaken hellscape. Cursing the heavens for his dismal fate, Upham steeled himself for the coming trial, his final stop on the summer circuit. Ruthless efficiency and detachment were key. He would mete out swift justice, then return to the comfortable confines of his home in French Village, where his wife, children, and slaves awaited him.

As the carriage finally lurched into Dorchester, Upham got his first glimpse of the newly constructed courthouse. Maybe it was just his mood, but its construction struck him as somewhat slapdash and architecturally rather uninspired for a building of such prominent purpose. The edifice spanned forty-eight feet in length, thirty-two in width, rising two full storeys to include the courtroom and tavern. The jail, in which Babcock now languished, had been dug into the foundation, invisible from street level. All told, it was unremarkable, although Upham thought the tavern was a nice touch.

Underwhelmed, Upham sighed and ordered his driver — a new slave bought to replace the recently executed Luke Hamilton — to drive on.

privilegium clericale [law Latin, "the benefits of clergy"] A historical provision under English law that allowed clergymen to claim they were exempt from the jurisdiction of civil courts by Divine authority ["touch not Mine anointed"].

A Fork to the Head

Aha! Aha! Aha! It was permitted!
— Amos Babcock, 1805[1]

Although the veracity of Reynolds's 1898 article remains questionable, one quotation contained within its pages is indirectly supported by another more credible source. In his pre-trial notes for the case, the prosecutor wrote that Babcock "might have thought under his delusion, that he was doing right, *as he express'd himself to Hanington*."[2] Even if the words attributed to Babcock were incorrect, it appears the sentiment was accurate. That sentiment — that the killing was somehow sanctioned or justified — was now the sole basis of Amos Babcock's defence.

How Amos came to the mistaken notion that the killing "was permitted" warrants further consideration, and all signs point to Jacob Peck. Peck's prophesy, conveyed through Amos's own daughter, was the spark that ignited Babcock's mania. Peck, supposedly channelling the spirit of John the Baptist, decreed unto Babcock, as the self-proclaimed Angel Gabriel, that the End of Days was nigh, that Mercy herself could not be saved, but that in death, she was destined to deliver Amos and his family to their Heavenly Father. Babcock, in his delirium, had taken Peck's prophesy literally, as nothing short of a Divine commandment.

This leads us to the issue of Divine authority. In Babcock's fevered mind, God's laws superseded those of man. God had spoken to Amos — albeit through Peck by way of his daughter — and Babcock felt powerless to defy God's will. Furthermore, with Judgment Day so close at hand, Babcock likely had little concern for whatever earthly punishment Mercy's death might incur.

There was a further element to Babcock's extraordinary leap of faith, one that also ineluctably came from Jacob Peck. In the courts of the British colonies in the late eighteenth century, the laws of God and man collided in a far more tangible way. Thanks to archaic law, there existed a little-known provision — *privilegium clericale* — commonly referred to as the "benefits of clergy."[3] The provision was a holdover from the earliest tribunals, when clerics were outside the jurisdiction of the secular courts, electing instead to be tried in ecclesiastical courts under canon law. As centuries passed and the legal system evolved, the benefits of clergy were radically modified. Eventually, the provision was no longer the sole bastion of the clergy, but had reached the stage where any first-time offender could invoke the benefits to have his sentence reduced. Consigned to the legal dustbin, the provision had long been nothing more than an obscure legal codicil, unheard of by the unwashed masses. All that changed when a highly publicized murder trial in the novice province of New Brunswick brought the benefits of clergy to the public's attention.

The killing took place in the fall of 1784 in Parr Town, a nefarious part of Saint John located south of Union Street. The victim — John Mosely, a black labourer — was killed by his wife Nancy in a jealous fit of pique. Liquor might have played a role. During their evening meal, without warning or provocation, Nancy stabbed John in the head with a fork. The wound did not prove instantly fatal. Mosely languished for almost a month before finally succumbing to his injuries.

In his report, coroner Samuel Moore wrote: "Agreeable to your request, I examined the black man's head. I am perfectly satisfied he was murdered. After examining where the fork perforated the temporal bones of the skull, I sawed off the arch of the head and found the brain everywhere impacted with matter. The symptoms before death were also very obvious. All the jury were spectators."[4] The coroner's jury, having endured the bloody autopsy, concurred. Amos Sheffield, foreman of the jury, declared "that the fork was the occasion of his death."[5] Death by fork was rare, even in 1784, and the trial attracted a considerable, if sometimes snickering, crowd. Nancy Mosely was indicted and brought to the bar, charged with murder. She was found guilty. Although no defendants were ever permitted to speak in their own defence during trial, tradition held that those convicted be asked if they had anything to say before sentence was imposed. Nancy Mosely stunned the court by invoking *privilegium clericale*. As a first-time offender, the court had little choice but to accept her defence, reducing her sentence to the lesser charge of manslaughter.[6]

The benefits of clergy extended even to her punishment. Originally destined for the hangman's noose, she was instead sentenced to be branded in open court with a hot iron. On the judge's instruction, before a riveted capacity crowd, the executioner burned the letter M onto the brawn of her left thumb. When the smoke cleared, her punishment was complete and she was free to go. The pain and public shame of the branding were not its sole purpose. At the time, there was no centralized system of criminal records. The brand allowed law enforcement in any jurisdiction to recognize repeat offenders.

The case ignited a media firestorm, to the extent possible in a town with only two newspapers. The lenient sentence sparked passionate debate as to the role of Divine authority in the newly established Supreme Court of New Brunswick, which had been granted its charter less than a month after the trial and branding of Nancy Mosely.[7] Although the scandal proved a boon to newspaper sales, the intricacies of the case and the archaic legal provision at its heart left editors struggling. As a result, reporting of the case tended toward the pedantic. Such gross oversimplifications left the public with the mistaken impression that those charged with murder could get off with a mere branding, simply by invoking the benefits of clergy.

Mosely's sentence was the talk of New Brunswick throughout 1785. Amos Babcock did not arrive in the province until 1791. Jacob Peck, on the other hand, had been living in Hillsborough since 1783. While it is unlikely Babcock had first-hand knowledge of the case, there is little chance Peck was not privy to the endless public debates incited by Mosely's branding. Coincidently, it is immediately after the Mosely trial that Peck "received his calling" and began to declare himself a preacher. Even if Peck failed to inform Amos Babcock directly of the benefits of clergy, it likely coloured the preacher's own perceptions of how local courts would treat the religiously devout accused of murder. Peck was playing with fire, labouring under the false belief that the courts looked sparingly on clerics.

Although the Mosely case received considerable media coverage, its fallout went unreported. Unbeknownst to Peck or Babcock, the Legislature of New Brunswick had modified the *privilegium clericale* provision in 1789, largely in response to the Mosely case. The trial had been an embarrassment for the fledgling court, if for no other reason than that the higher courts had abolished branding in 1779, a full six years before it was used in the Mosely case. The modified clause still allowed judges to offer some leniency to first-time offenders charged with lesser offences, but no longer afforded blanket immunity to clerics or those accused of capital crimes. The debate raged on as the courts fought to separate church and state, as well as rid themselves of lingering public misperceptions regarding the benefits of clergy. The loophole closed forever when *privilegeum clericale* was stricken from English law in 1827.

All this legal wrangling was lost on Amos Babcock. Without the benefits of clergy, his defence options were limited. He could not reasonably argue the killing had been in self-defence. And regardless of what others thought, Amos did not think himself mad and would not cop to an insanity plea. As his trial approached, his lone remaining defence was his ardent belief that he had done what he thought was right in the eyes of God, if not in those of man. Whether Amos Babcock could tell right from wrong — one of the key diagnostics in the legal definition of insanity — was a question very much on the mind of the man recently appointed as chief prosecutor in the case: Ward Chipman, Esquire.

Of Traitors and Tribulations

Ward Chipman[1]

As the trials of Amos Babcock and Jacob Peck loomed large on the horizon, Ward Chipman Sr. was in the prime of his life. Fifty-one years of age, distinguished, balding, and stout, he embraced his avuncular appearance, using it to lull many an unsuspecting adversary into a false sense of complacency. Crafty by choice and ruthless of necessity, Chipman was unquestionably at the top of his profession. He brought to the court a wealth of experience and an impeccable reputation. He was renowned for his calm reasoning, concise arguments, and encyclopedic knowledge of the law. Peck and Babcock never stood a chance.

In the summer of 1805, Chipman Sr. was serving as the Solicitor General of New Brunswick. He had travelled from England in 1784 to assume the post. Despite his brief stint in London, Chipman was an American, born in Massachusetts in 1754.[2] There, he trained as a lawyer before assuming the alliterative title of deputy muster master general of the Provincial Forces at New York. Other military posts soon followed, including serving as an advocate of the Admiralty Court and commissioner to receive claims for supplies. Anxious to trade the military for the law, Ward Chipman criss-crossed the Atlantic in pursuit of opportunity and advancement.

Despite his early roving years, Chipman had settled nicely into the role of Solicitor General. The cases of Babcock and Peck were by no means Chipman's most demanding to date. He had seen his fair share of high-profile trials in the past, including that of the notorious Benedict Arnold, whom Chipman successfully represented before none other than the implacable Judge Joshua Upham. Barrister Chipman was equally confident he would prove victorious against the seditious Mr. Peck. Arnold — the American general who famously had defected to the British after his plot to surrender the fort under his command was exposed — had moved to Saint John at the end of the Revolutionary War. There, he and his son Richard established a trading company in 1786, partnering with Monson Hayt, a Loyalist and justice of the peace for York County. Incorporating with a single ship, the firm began importing from the West Indies. The company was hardly a mercantile force, however, surrounded by fleets of larger, more profitable competitors. Business soon floundered and the partnership grew increasingly adversarial.

It was not long before Arnold caused a scandal in Saint John. In 1789 his fledgling company filed several lawsuits against its debtors, and Arnold himself sued the eminent lawyer Edward Winslow. The stress of the pending legal actions and a decline in trade prompted Hayt and Arnold to dissolve their now acrimonious partnership, and the pair soon became embroiled in a complicated series of suits and counter-suits. Arnold had lent Hayt significant sums of money, and Hayt's promissory notes proved worthless. Arnold filed yet another suit against Hayt, hoping to use the courts to reclaim some of the monies owed. Arnold eventually prevailed, and for his efforts was awarded a little over £2,500. Soon after, a fire destroyed the store owned by Arnold and Hayt.

All the legal squabbling was merely a precursor to the main event. Hayt, arguably in an act of retaliation, alleged that Arnold had deliberately sparked the blaze to claim some insurance money. Arnold fired back, suing Hayt for slander. The corporate mudslinging, coupled with Arnold's infamy, soon had the public in a frenzy. Benedict Arnold hired the city's top legal mind — Ward Chipman Sr. — to represent him in the matter, along with fellow barrister Jonathon Bliss.

The trial of *Arnold v. Hayt* took place on September 7, 1791, before Supreme Court justices Isaac Allen and Joshua Upham.[3] Thanks in no small part to Chipman's inflammatory summation, the jury found Hayt guilty of slander. Arnold's victory, however, was tinged with insult. The jury, sickened by the childish antics of the opposing parties and the lingering taint of Arnold's treasonous past, awarded him a mere twenty shillings in damages. Morally affronted, Arnold returned to England, where he died a decade later. Even in death, Arnold could not escape his most famous transgression. In the centuries that followed, Benedict Arnold's name became synonymous with "traitor." For his part, Ward Chipman cared more for the notoriety of the case than for the duplicitous man at its heart.

As the Crown's cases against Babcock and Peck found their way onto the impressively sprawling and intricately carved desk of Ward Chipman, the Solicitor General was spoiling for another contentious public brawl. The strange events in the backwater of Shediac seemed tailor-made for a litigator with a secret taste for the limelight. Peck was a preacher charged with blasphemy. Babcock stood accused of killing his sister in a religious frenzy. Ward Chipman never backed away from a fight, particularly one destined for the front page.

If Chipman's past had earned him the right to argue before the highest court in the province, his future would soon see the roles reversed. Within three years, Chipman's temperament and skill would win him his own spot on the bench of the New Brunswick Supreme Court. Appointed the Honourable Ward Chipman, he sat in judgment for fifteen years, retiring in April 1823 to accept an even higher honour, becoming the first administrator of New Brunswick. By then, Justice Chipman's love of the law had become a family affair. His son, Ward Chipman Jr., replaced him on the bench, eventually rising to the rank of chief justice of the Supreme Court, a post he held from 1834 to 1851. It was a fitting end to a legal dynasty that helped shape the course of jurisprudence in the coastal province.

Chipman's future and that of his progeny were undeniably bright in June 1805. The only things standing in the way were a couple of illiterate yeomen who had wreaked havoc on a tiny hamlet on the eastern shore. Despite the public's momentary interest in the pair, Ward Chipman had little doubt the cases would be tried, resolved, and forgotten in no time.

ei incumbit probatio qui dicit, non qui negat
[Latin, "the proof lies upon the one who affirms, not upon the one who denies"] The presumption of innocence until proven guilty, a legal right of the accused in a criminal trial; the burden falls to the prosecutor to prove guilt, not to the defendant to prove innocence.

Indefensible

Those reared on a steady diet of twentieth-century American crime dramas might be surprised to learn that the oft-cited edict, "if you cannot afford a lawyer, one will be provided to you free of charge,"[1] is a foreign concept in Canadian law. Even today, those accused of serious crimes in Canada are not entitled to gratis defence counsel, unlike their American counterparts.[2] In 1805 the idea of a public defender would have been laughable.

The misconception has led a few historians to report erroneously that Amos Babcock chose to defend himself at trial. That is not technically correct, but it is accurate to say that Babcock appeared *pro se*, with no lawyer to defend him. In nineteenth-century criminal trials conducted under British (and by extension New Brunswick) law, the accused was not entitled to be represented by counsel. The reasoning behind the law was simple: there was a legal presumption of innocence, and the burden of proof rested entirely with the prosecution. The law thus did not require a proactive defence and often would not allow one, although those of means were not always content to leave their fate in the hands of the jury. By that point in history, the wealthy were engaging private counsel when the necessity arose, which it rarely did in a system that favoured the rich. The rules for the indigent, however, would not change until the Prisoner's Counsel Act of 1836. Accordingly, Jacob Peck and Amos Babcock were little more than pawns in a legal game that took place almost despite them.

Amos Babcock, charged with the far more egregious crime of murder, quickly became the Crown's focus, no doubt to the delight of Jacob Peck. Chances are it was the only time in his life the imperious preacher was content to yield the spotlight. The burden of proving Babcock's guilt fell squarely on the ample shoulders of Ward Chipman. As Chipman had no way of knowing what defence Babcock might present, the prosecutor had little choice but to prepare for every contingency.

Ward Chipman was good enough to leave behind a very concise road map to his thinking. His pre-trial notes, outlining his opening arguments to the jury, reveal that Chipman clearly had done his homework.[3] Point by point, the Solicitor-General-turned-chief-prosecutor stood ready to shoot down any and all of Babcock's possible pleas for leniency.

To start, Chipman dismissed alcohol as a mitigating factor, proclaiming "drunkenness is no excuse."[4] Counter to modern sensibilities, however, Chipman allowed: "tho' it may make a man so mad, that he knows not what he does"[5] — a sentiment against which prosecutors have argued stridently in the centuries since. Nowhere in the litany of witness statements was there even the suggestion Babcock had imbibed any intoxicants on the night in question, or on any other night for that matter. Still, Chipman had the argument standing by, should the issue be raised in court. Ward Chipman was not a man who enjoyed surprises.

With intoxication ruled out, Chipman then shifted his attention to the possibility Babcock might plead insanity. It was Babcock's best line of defence, one the prosecutor intended to render moot. On this one count, Chipman had the weight of the law in his favour. Contrary to popular notions of what constitutes "crazy," the legal definition of insanity codifies a common law test for mental disorder. To be deemed legally insane, the accused must show evidence of "a mental disorder that rendered the person incapable of appreciating the nature and quality of the act... or of knowing that it was wrong."[6] The test specifically excludes self-induced states caused by alcohol and drugs or transitory mental states such as hysteria or delusion.

Chipman believed Amos failed the common law test. "If insanity is his defense," wrote Chipman, "he must show a total alienation of mind... that he has not voluntarily brought it upon himself."[7] He later elaborated on the thought: "Madness... whether permanent or temporary must be unequivocal & plain — not an idle frantic humour or unaccountable mode of action but an *absolute dispossession* of the free and natural agency of the human mind."[8] Chipman closed his argument by reminding the jurors that, "in all very atrocious crimes there must be supposed a degree of derangement of mind,"[9] imploring them not to confuse the inherently irrational act of murder with being insane.

Chipman reserved his harshest condemnation, and the majority of his opening statement, to Babcock's more likely defence strategy: religious infatuation. By this stage, New Brunswick law had severely curtailed the benefits of clergy. Claiming exemption on religious grounds was no longer the free pass it had once been. Still, religion permeated all aspects of society, including the court. Chipman knew that to dismiss all religious doctrine outright might alienate the devout members of the jury. Instead, the prosecutor elected to focus the jury's attention on the fallacious nature of the religious dogma in this particular case.

Chipman honed his attack, breaking the complex and all-encompassing notion of religious belief into discrete parts, easily digestible by jurors. He opened boldly, discounting "any idle wild fanatic opinion that a man may be so in a state of grace, that no act he commits can be attended with guilt."[10] He then appealed to the piety of the jurors themselves, praising religious principles while condemning those who misused them: "It is astonishing that the mild religion of the Gospel the Christian revelation designed, to give peace on earth and goodwill to mankind, should ever be so perverted and abused as to give rise to a doctrine calculated to reduce mankind to savages."[11] Chipman now found himself on the razor's edge, forced to concede that the sacred Scriptures sometimes led men to expect and accept some delusions as part and parcel of having faith. Dancing along the finest of lines, Ward deftly balanced the conflicting demands of challenging Babcock's delusions while simultaneously stopping short of ridiculing the deeply held, if somewhat irrational, religious convictions of the panel.

Unlike his predecessor, William Botsford, prosecutor Chipman recognized the role Jacob Peck and his mountebank ministry had played in Babcock's actions. Throughout his opening remarks, Chipman acknowledged the fallacy of Peck's harangues. Chipman called both Babcock and the accursed preacher to task, writing: "If ignorant and weak minds by indulging in reveries of this kind, imbibe such principles and act upon them, *however conscientious they may pretend to be*, they must be answerable for all their conduct and suffer the punishment of their crimes."[12] Chipman never hedged, recognizing Peck and his prophesies for what they were: "with regard to those whose coming is after the working of Satan — because they received not the love of the truth that they might be saved — for this cause God shall send them strong delusion, that *they should believe a lie*."[13]

The prosecutor, having crafted his opening marks, was ready for battle. The evidence against Babcock was overwhelming. As Chipman headed to the courthouse, he was confident he could establish guilt beyond all reasonable doubt. Whatever defence Babcock might eschew, Chipman had a rebuttal honed and at hand.

The prosecutor also planned to kill two birds with a single stone. In revealing the instigating prophesies to be falsehoods, Chipman would destroy both Babcock and Peck.

Act 5 The Preamble

act 6
Justice Done

Merits and Demerits

Every popular account of the Babcock tragedy reports that Amos's trial was held on June 15, 1805. In truth, it began on Thursday, June 13.[1] For on that day, Judge Joshua Upham gavelled into session the first *Nisi Prius* Court of Westmorland County to be held in the recently donated, politically motivated Dorchester Courthouse. The Honourable Amos Botsford was seated as his associate justice, his son William nowhere in sight. Botsford was joined by his fellow county magistrates James Law, Charles Dixon, and Samuel Gay. Upham liked nothing more than to hold court surrounded by lesser legal luminaries. Hezekiah King resumed his role as clerk of the court, tasked with keeping a record of the trial proceedings.

Upham began by revisiting some well-trodden ground. Although a grand jury had already heard the evidence against Amos Babcock prior to his indictment, Justice Upham decided to empanel another grand jury to review the case. This time, experience trumped nepotism. Solicitor General Ward Chipman would present the Crown's case. Mindful of the slight afforded his son, Amos Botsford swallowed the insult without comment.

A twenty-man jury was sworn and settled into the closed courtroom. In a further deviation from the prior panel, this jury would hear testimony directly from the witnesses themselves. In a final break from the previous proceeding, only three witnesses were sworn to give testimony: Jonathon

Babcock, Samuel Cornwall, and Amasa Killam. Chipman offered no explanation as to why other key witnesses, including Babcock's wife Dorcas or William Hanington, were not called.

No trial transcript was recorded, at least not as we understand it today. Clerk King noted only the witness appearances and the outcome; writing longhand with quill and ink, he did not have the luxury of entering the specifics of their testimony, although it presumably mirrored their written depositions. After the three witnesses recounted the events in question, Upham's tender joints begged for relief and the court was adjourned. Amos Babcock had yet to set foot in the courtroom.

The next day, Friday, June 14, the grand jury was again duly sworn and seated. For reasons not specified, four additional members were added to the panel. Despite having missed the previous day's testimony, the late additions were sworn in just in time for the main attraction. The accused — Amos Babcock — was at last brought before the bar. Shadowed by his jailer, Robert Keillor, the prisoner shuffled into the dock, looking ragged and unkempt. In sonorous tones intended to carry well beyond the courtroom walls, Justice Upham read the indictment against him, then asked for his plea. Babcock, with no counsel to guide him, replied "not guilty." The very model of swift justice, Upham ordered Babcock to stand trial the next day. Amos was then led back to his perdition below the floorboards.

Although by far the one with the highest profile, Babcock's murder trial was not the only matter before the court that day. All higher crimes outside the jurisdictional scope of the Westmorland magistrates were remanded to the *nisi prius* court. Joshua Upham, short on patience and in visible discomfort from his arthritis, peevishly dispensed with numerous bits of judicial housekeeping. The judge then called the next case on the docket, *The Crown v. Jerome*.

The accused, the personification of a career criminal, was brought before the bar. Shifty-eyed and wily, the prisoner smirked as he faced his accusers. The case was a relatively simple matter, the kind Upham happily would have left to his local brethren to adjudicate. The accused, John Jerome, allegedly had stolen some small items from a gentleman, James

Law. The antithesis of Jerome, haughty to the point of caricature, Law took the stand as though the entire legal process was beneath his dignity. The aggrieved gentleman was duly sworn in, indignant at the notion any might ever doubt his word.

Before Law drew breath to testify, something truly unexpected occurred. Justice Upham called an abrupt halt to the proceedings. After more than forty-eight hours spent exiled in the bucolic netherworld that was Dorchester, Upham had reached his limit. It was apparent to all that the Honourable Joshua Upham had a far more pressing matter he needed to get off his chest.

The now twenty-four strong jury sat in curious silence. The panel consisted of the county's elite: landholders and freeholders, men of status, education, and influence. Upham could no longer resist the opportunity to address this exalted and captive audience on a matter of grave concern. In an unprecedented (and no doubt awkward) moment, Judge Upham berated the men of the jury "in a very pointed manner upon the badness of the public roads and bridges through the county and the impossibility of passing them without danger to travelers and their horses."[2]

The judge's screed shocked the staid jurors. Having already abandoned all sense of decorum and tradition, court clerk King took a moment to transcribe the judge's rebuke into the court minutes. Suitably chastised, the members of the jury had little choice but to weather Upham's storm. What had prompted such opprobrium eluded all who witnessed it. Perhaps Law's self-important swagger proved the tipping point, the catalyst that ignited Upham's barely contained ire.

Then, as suddenly as it began, the judge's tirade ceased. Upham, having vented his spleen, gavelled the court back into session. Utterly deflated, Law haltingly testified as to the robbery. Equally flustered, the jury voted unanimously to indict the accused, never once looking up to meet the eye of their unstable overlord for fear of sparking another outburst.

Despite the time lost to recriminations and district-wide abasements, the wheels of justice continued to turn, and at last the day's docket cleared. Justice Upham adjourned the court in a manner that invited no further discussion or debate. The dinner hour was fast approaching, and given the appalling state of the roads, it would take him some time to return to the inn. He would undoubtedly be dining alone.

The grand jury — having exercised its civic duty and been soundly berated for its lack of civic pride — was dismissed with the measured thanks and heartfelt condemnation of the court.

Plea in Suspension

Just before 11:00 a.m. on Saturday, June 15, 1805, clerk Hezekiah King strode into the packed courtroom and bade those assembled to rise. With difficulty, Judge Joshua Upham sat himself behind the bench, his previous day's outburst regarding the roads and bridges forgotten in the light of more pressing concerns. He was soon joined by his stable of associate and junior magistrates, an intimidating phalanx of robed judiciaries. The expectant crowd fell silent, eager to witness the social events of the season: the trials of Amos Babcock and Jacob Peck.[1]

Upham called the court into session. The bench's first order of business was to seat a petit jury. It was not a daunting task. The voir dire process of jury selection in 1805 bore little resemblance to the judicial blood sport we know today, in which every potential panel member is scrutinized and rejected for seemingly trivial causes. Judge Upham was handed a list of prospective jurors, a pool of twenty-six names. Included among their ranks were the brother of a crucial prosecution witness and a man named Peck, although he claimed no direct relation to the accused. Sight unseen, the judge drew the following jury: Aaron Brownell, his brother Jeremiah, Bill Chappell, Daniel Gooden, Christopher Carter, Thomas Easterbrooks, Thomas Bowser, Oliver Barnes, Eliphalet Read, John Dobson, and John Chapman. William Trueman was elected jury foreman, his sole qualification being the clarity and precision of his handwriting.

For the sake of expediency, Upham elected to clear the lesser cases from the day's docket. First up, the matter of the preacher charged with blasphemy. After some preliminary opening remarks, Ward Chipman began the proceedings by swearing in William Hanington, Dorcas Babcock, and Amasa Killam. Each testified, Hanington taking the bulk of the allotted time. The transcript of the February 12 revival was read aloud as it was entered into evidence, replete with its apocryphal prophesies. Hanington described how Peck's aberrant services had laid siege to the town, transforming once sane neighbours into nihilists and catatonics. Satisfied he had met his burden of proof, Chipman rested the prosecution's case.

The defendant was then called before the bar. Jacob Peck swept into the court, resplendent in his gentleman's coat and obsequious in his greetings to the bench. The feckless preacher's day of reckoning was at hand, although his demeanour was one of certainty, not fear. Despite the circumstances, Peck seemed to relish being the centre of attention. He stood solemnly, his head unbowed, as the charges against him were read to the court. When asked, Peck pleaded not guilty to all counts.

Ward Chipman sat in bemused silence, curious to see how this blithe charlatan would evade responsibility for his actions. He did not have long to wait. The preacher, serving as his own defence counsel, stunned Chipman, the bench, and the court by declaring he was not ready to stand trial "on account of the absence of material witnesses."[2] The court minutes do not record who these crucial witnesses were or why they were unavailable. Since everyone relevant to the case was already assembled in the courtroom, waiting to testify in the Babcock trial, Peck's missing witnesses must have been character testimonials of some sort. Alternatively, the delay was merely a ploy on Peck's part to buy time and await the outcome of Amos's trial.

Even more shocking was that Upham allowed the motion, although not without extracting some measure of penance. The judge agreed to grant the continuance provided Peck agreed to pay an additional £200 bond. Furthermore, Upham demanded Peck produce two additional guarantors. Having clearly anticipated such an outcome, Peck had his

sureties at the ready. At Peck's command, two men — Daniel McDonald and Henry Steeves — approached the bench and swore the necessary oaths.[3] Upham levied a separate bond of £100 against each man and made them both affirm to the court that they would ensure Peck returned to face his charges during its next session.

The identities of Peck's second set of sureties mirrored his first. One man, Henry Steeves, had obvious ties to Peck. The two were neighbours from Salisbury. Steeves, a well-regarded Baptist preacher, was from an established and respected family. That he was willing to stand up for Peck lent the accused some much-needed credibility, even as it damaged Steeves's own reputation. The other surety, Daniel McDonald, is an enigma. Like Reuben Mills, one of Peck's first guarantors, Daniel McDonald had no prior relationship with Peck. More troubling is the complete absence of anyone named Daniel McDonald in the district's civic records — no trace of the man can be found in the census; town books; birth, death, marriage, or land registries; or other local records. Odds are Daniel McDonald, like Mills, was a bondsman, a mercenary hired to vouch for a man who could find no one among his acquaintances to endorse him.

With £400 newly added to its coffers, the court postponed Peck's trial until the fall session. With excessive flourish, Peck bid farewell to the court and took his leave. It is not known whether he lingered in the courthouse or joined the spectators in the gallery to watch the trial of his one-time acolyte Amos Babcock. Peck was under no obligation to stay, despite his key role in the events leading up to the murder of Mercy Hall. As the preacher did not appear on the witness lists for either the prosecution or the defence in *The Crown v. Amos Babcock*, he could not be called to testify. The court would hear no further from Jacob Peck that day. It would, however, hear a great deal about him.

The Burden of Proof

Courthouse spectators, drawn in hopes of bearing witness to unprecedented legal theatrics and the scandalous details of the county's most notorious crime, sat disheartened and frustrated. Tales of Peck's hellfire revivals and outlandish declarations had the crowd on tenterhooks, primed for some truly incandescent courtroom antics by the manic preacher. What they saw instead was a phlegmatic exchange, devoid of drama or intrigue. Their only hope of satiety now lay with Babcock and the grisly particulars of his crime. Those gallery denizens craving scurrilous spectacle would be sorely tested by an obdurate magistrate with his own agenda.

Determined to dispense with all pending irritants before giving the crowd what it wanted, Judge Upham returned to the case of the recently indicted burglar, John Jerome.[1] Upham's rantings had derailed the prior day's proceedings, and the judge sought to expiate his lapse in professional conduct by setting the case to rights. Jerome was escorted to the bar and the indictment against him was read. Unbeknownst to any in the courtroom, least of all the accused, Justice Upham had already decided the outcome of this case. Instead of asking Jerome for his plea, Upham declared that his trial would also be postponed, although unlike Peck, no future trial date was set. Bewildered, Jerome could scarcely believe this sudden reversal of fortune. Without further explanation, the prisoner was led away by Robert Keillor, back to the manacles that awaited him in the dungeon. For reasons that will soon become clear, the court records regarding the fate of John Jerome were purposefully left vague.

With no other impediments to the cause, the Honourable Joshua Upham moved to the day's headline attraction, *The Crown v. Amos Babcock.*

Ward Chipman, true to his carefully crafted plan of attack, made his opening statements to the jury in plumy tones, burnished by years of courthouse oratory. The prosecutor welcomed jurors and reminded them of their solemn sworn duty, then, segueing seamlessly into the case at hand, Chipman told the esteemed panel he was not a man given to emotional rhetoric. As was his custom, Chipman intended to let the evidence speak for itself. Scanning their riveted and expectant faces, he declared, "I shall make no comments upon the facts after they are given in evidence — this will be the Province of the Court."[2] As for the evidence, Chipman assured those assembled, it was bountiful, irrefutable, and damning.

Bountiful though the evidence might have been, it consisted entirely of eyewitness testimony, an inherently emotional and therefore suspect line of inquiry. Undaunted by the limitations of his case, Chipman called Jonathon Babcock to the stand. If Jonathon's courtroom testimony was half as graphic and sanguinary as his written statement, the gore-hungry spectators would finally get their first taste of their long-sought quarry. By all accounts, Jonathon did not disappoint. He regaled the court with a re-enactment of the crime that would not soon be forgotten.

The ravenous hordes temporarily sated, Chipman now found himself in dire emotional straits, a position he had promised the jury only moments before to avoid at all costs. According to his pre-trial notes, Chipman meant to use Jonathon's testimony to call into question the character of the victim herself. In a single cryptic note, Chipman alluded to "the supposed former grudge," which he planned to introduce "*with caution.*"[3] The nature of the grudge can only be inferred from the context — likely some simmering filial resentment from years past.

It was a risky strategy for Chipman. The prosecution's case held that Amos had killed Mercy in a fit of religious zeal. To suggest there was a far more pedestrian motivation for the killing — some long-harboured sibling rivalry or slight — ran the risk of muddying the waters, potentially

crippling the prosecution's argument. It is not clear from the existing minutes of the court whether Chipman introduced the siblings' ancient history as part of his case. What is evident from his notes is that he intended to blame the victim, a reprehensible ploy normally reserved for desperate defence lawyers. Key to Chipman's character assassination was "that the deceased was considered a reprobate,"[4] implying Mercy somehow had incited her own murder with her slothful, indolent behaviour. In hindsight, the smear campaign appears as unnecessary as it was ill-conceived. One can only hope Chipman exercised caution and opted for the higher ground, abandoning the plan *in toto*. Whatever its content, when Chipman's line of questioning was exhausted, Jonathon was dismissed.

Having successfully established the physical elements of the crime, Chipman now focused on the accused's behaviour in the days surrounding the killing. To lay the groundwork, Chipman called William Hanington to the stand to relay the story of the neglected cattle, as well as Amos's aberrant conduct at the revivals. Chipman was also hoping to elicit a specific quotation, manoeuvring Hanington to repeat Babcock's declaration that the killing "was permitted."[5] With Amos's pre-crime angst duly noted, Chipman then imposed on Amasa Killam to recount Babcock's unhinged demeanour in the hours and days following the murder.

Satisfied he had painted Babcock as a reckless miscreant capable of murder, Chipman changed tack. The prosecutor unleashed the third prong of his strategy, effectively pre-empting any effort by Babcock to claim the insanity defence. To this end, Chipman summoned in turn Samuel Cornwall and Lucy Bramble to the witness stand to share their recollections of the revival held hours before Mercy was slaughtered. For the second time, the jury and gallery heard the specifics of the apocalyptic prophesies and fables of winged redemption that ostensibly were the motive for murder.

As Lucy Bramble exited the courtroom, Chipman recalled one key revivalist, Amasa Killam. Like Cornwall and Bramble before him, Killam captivated jurors with tales of Peck's month-long diatribes of doom and personal greetings from the king. Chipman then directed the witness's attention to the search for Mercy's body. Killam had headed the search party and had been among those who unearthed her makeshift tomb of ice and snow. His recounting of the macabre scene no doubt thrilled spectators, but Chipman's questions had purpose beyond eliciting sensationalist fodder. He wanted the jury to hear both how Amos hid the body — the evidence of his crime — and how he systematically erased his own footprints in the snow, sweeping away the telltale signs of his misdeed with an evergreen bough. Surely, Chipman reminded the jury, such deliberate and reasoned attempts to conceal the crime were proof positive Babcock knew his actions were wrong at the time of the offence — the cornerstone in the legal definition of sanity. Having successfully raised the spectre of Babcock's feigned madness, Chipman excused his witness, thanking him profusely for his service to the court.

Chipman was a consummate showman and true craftsman. When it came to the question of Babcock's mental state, Chipman saved his master stroke for last, ensuring maximum impact. The chief prosecutor called a now-familiar face to the stand: the Dorchester Courthouse's own jailer, Robert Keillor. Despite Keillor's reputation for drink and the immediate proximity of his tavern to the proceedings, he was from a proud and distinguished family. Whatever his inebriated condition off-hours, Keillor took the stand soberly and with all due solemnity. He was well aware it fell to him to deliver the prosecution's knockout punch.

Keillor was called for one purpose: to inform the jury of the "accidental discovery"[6] he made during Babcock's incarceration in the cellar dungeon. We likely will never know what he said. To date, it remains an exasperating void in the case file that the nature of this discovery was not recorded for posterity. No details appear in either the court minutes or the media account of the trial. Keillor never committed his fateful observations to paper in any of his later correspondence. What he witnessed cannot be surmised from any existing sources, yet the power of his testimony is evident in the outcome. Whatever Keillor saw, it was sufficient to convince the jury that Babcock was a malingerer.

Having met his prosecutorial burden — firmly establishing the *acteus reus* and *mens rea* necessary to prove guilt — Chipman made an unusual decision. Despite his prior protestations, he elected to rest his case on an

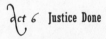

emotional note. For his final witness, Chipman called the wife of the accused, Dorcas Babcock. It was a bold move in that she was not needed to confirm any facts in the case. The content of her testimony had been covered previously by Jonathon, a fellow eyewitness to Amos's descent into madness. Prior witnesses had also provided ample commentary on Amos's behaviour before and after the crime. Dorcas's testimony was redundant, but Chipman understood the emotional power of her taking the stand. As Chipman no doubt made clear to the jury, the law did not require her to do so, and the prosecutor gambled that her decision to forgo convention and testify against her husband spoke to the defendant's guilt. It was a message Chipman wanted the jurors to hear.

Chipman's decision to subpoena Dorcas was not his only controversial call. Those excluded from the prosecution's witness list were as significant as those included, if not more so. Notable in their absence were the Poirier brothers — Joseph Jr. and Peter — whose brawn helped fetter a raving and absconding Babcock in the hours following the crime. Language barriers and institutionalized prejudice kept the Acadians off the stand, thanks in no small part to coroner Gideon Palmer, tasked with identifying key witnesses for the Crown. Since the coroner failed to interview them during his inquest, Chipman had little way of knowing their involvement in pivotal events.

Far more contentious was the glaring omission of Jacob Peck. Chipman's choice to call Lucy Bramble, William Hanington, Amasa Killam, and Samuel Cornwall to testify about the revival indicates the prosecutor understood the significance of the prophesies to the crime. Why Chipman opted not to question the preacher himself remains one of the great mysteries of the case. Was it that Chipman recognized Peck as a pathological liar, incapable of honesty even under oath? As Peck stood indicted for multiple felonies, he was far from a credible witness. Or did the prosecutor fear Peck might commandeer the witness stand as a soapbox pulpit, monopolizing the court to advance his own twisted agenda? It might have been as simple as a technicality. Defendants were prohibited from testifying in their own defence, and, as Peck stood indicted on unrelated charges, Chipman may have erred on the side of caution, electing to keep the preacher off the stand altogether.

Whatever his reasoning, the composition of Chipman's witness list represents one of the few missteps in an otherwise compelling performance.

Unable or unwilling to call the preacher, Ward Chipman settled for the accused's spouse. Even if she were overcome with emotion, Dorcas proved a safer bet than Peck. Though the sisters-in-law had lived at odds, forced to coexist in a mutually toxic state of depression and resentment, Dorcas at last came to Mercy's defence. Her words were as damning as they were heart-rending. On February 13, as her husband laid waste to what little they had built together, Dorcas stood by as a sixpenny knife slashed her fragile world to tatters. She had done nothing to save Mercy in the moment. She now took the stand, resolute and defiant, hoping to find some small measure of redemption by condemning Mercy's killer. The gallery, having had their fill of viscera, now feasted on the rage, confusion, and devastation that were at the heart of the story.

As Dorcas Babcock stepped down, the prosecution rested its case. Though not entirely true to his word regarding emotion, Chipman had let the facts speak for themselves. Despite a last passionate gasp, he had shown remarkable restraint in presenting the case, forsaking grandstanding for a more measured approach. All eyes now turned to the accused, Amos Babcock.

In this hopelessly lopsided fight, David was understandably awestruck by his opposing Goliath. Babcock had never before set foot in a courtroom, much less been responsible for crafting his own defence. In the judicial age of the "Bloody Code," when even minor infractions were punishable by death, Amos found himself at the base of a lethally sharp learning curve.

To his credit, Amos Babcock did not go down without a fight, nor did he claim insanity. As with all delusionals, Amos was incapable of recognizing his illness or of acknowledging his dogmatic religious convictions as fantasies. He did not perceive himself as insane, nor would he abase himself as such, even to save his own life. He could never deny the power of the Lord. Amos's spiritual beliefs might have been unsubstantiated, but such is the nature of faith. For all Chipman's well-honed precautions, Babcock never raised the issue of insanity in his own defence.

Amos's defence strategy was the soul of simplicity. He persisted in his

claim that the killing was justified by the prophesies.[7] To that end, Babcock called his first witness, his daughter Dorcas.[8] The teenager was not deposed during the coroner's inquest, nor had she been called to testify before the grand jury, possibly on account of her tender age. No written record of her statement survives. As such, the exact content of her testimony can be deduced only from the circumstances. She was likely called to recount her participation in the revival of February 12.

Like Chipman, Amos Babcock also elected not to call Jacob Peck to the witness stand. Perhaps Amos had finally accepted the truth about his malevolent pedagogue. Despite Peck's repeated proclamations, the world had not come to a fiery end as scheduled, at least not for anyone other than Mercy and now Amos. It is far more likely, however, that Babcock clung to his belief that the prophesy was genuine, delivered by God through his eldest child. For that reason alone, he chose Dorcas, rather than Peck, to testify as to the vision's veracity. Without question, the girl made a far more sympathetic and credible witness than Peck ever would.

Lacking any notion of the law or judicial strategy, Babcock called his second and final witness, John Welling. After all, the fateful revival had occurred at Welling's home. Perhaps fearing the jury might perceive his own daughter as a biased witness, Babcock sought to bolster the integrity of the prophesies by calling a respected member of the community, who had the added benefit of being an adult, male, and unrelated. What, if anything, Welling contributed to Babcock's defence died with the jurors — his testimony never entered the court record. Considering the outcome, it seems his appearance did little to sway the jury.

With the deck already stacked against him, Amos was further saddled with an erroneous perception rampant among juries of the era. It was a commonly held belief that committing a crime at night meant nefarious intent and a desire to avoid detection. This led countless juries to an automatic assumption of guilt on the part of any and all nighttime perpe-trators, regardless of the facts of the case. Darkness implied deceit and resolve. That Amos killed in full view of his family carried less weight with the jury than did the fact Babcock struck the fatal blow in the dead of night. Incomprehensible though it may seem, Amos would have fared better had he waited till daybreak to commit the heinous deed. Perhaps John Welling was called to counter this assumption, reinforcing for the less open-minded jurors that the act was not one of malice but rather one spawned of genuine religious conviction, however misguided.

As Welling stepped down, Amos found he had nothing more to say. The law did not permit him to speak for himself. The defence team of one rested. Amos had done his level best to save himself against a tidal wave of damning evidence. He could not and did not deny he committed the act. His lone hope of acquittal lay in convincing the jury he had acted in accordance with God's laws, irrespective of the laws of the land.

The totality of the trial — the testimony of eight witnesses, as well as opening and closing remarks — lasted less than six hours. The spectators' patience was repaid in horrifying splendour, an almost pornographic display of human depravity, religious zealotry, and madness. They would dine out on the graphic details for months. Anxious for the final act, the crowd grew restless. Sensing a meal and a respite from the voyeurism were in order, Upham checked the clock and adjourned the proceedings until six that evening. Hezekiah King ordered the court rise as the bench was cleared. Keillor, fresh from his star turn on the stand, restrained the prisoner and led him back to his cell. The jailer then raced up the stairs to greet his patrons, a teaming mass of spectators, jurors, and hangers-on converging on the tavern in search of spirits and speculation as to the upcoming verdict.

Before many in the crowd were able to down their drink, six bells sounded, and the hordes streamed en masse back into the gallery. As the court reconvened, Judge Upham had one last task at hand. With his customary brusqueness and brevity, he gave his final instructions to the jury, providing the legal definitions and sentencing guidelines necessary to reach a verdict. Chipman had little to add, opting to "leave the cause with confidence that the Jury will do right."[9] Suitably instructed, the jurors were sent to deliberate. A few in the gallery took the jury's departure as a sign to return to the pub. From long experience, Chipman and the bench elected to wait in situ, hopeful of a swift decision.

 Act 6 **Justice Done**

Those who ventured to the tavern had barely drained their first draught when the call rang out once again — the jury was back, the verdict was in. As one, the spectators raced through the courthouse stairwell, determined to regain their seats before the gavel dropped. Caught unawares, even the court clerk Hezekiah King scrambled to return in time. The jury had deliberated less than thirty minutes.

Such a quick verdict did not bode well for the accused. As the gallery settled, the jury hastily reassembled in the jury box and Upham called the court back into session. At the bench's urging, the foreman — William Trueman — announced the jury's unanimous decision: guilty as charged. With the possible exception of the accused, everyone present had predicted just such an outcome, and the verdict caused little uproar in the courtroom.

The Honourable Joshua Upham, visibly pleased with the jury's finding, continued pro forma. Amos, still reeling from his memento mori, was summoned to the bar. In a tone he reserved for those newly confronted with their own limited mortality, Upham asked Babcock if he had anything to say to the court before sentence was passed. An expectant hush descended over the courtroom. Traditionally, this was the moment when a defendant might invoke the benefits of clergy. Eyes locked to the floorboards beneath his feet, Amos Babcock remained silent. Affording the accused a suitable pause, Upham had his answer.

With that, the judge declared: "The sentence of the court is that you shall be taken hence to the place from whence you came, then to the place of execution, and there be hanged by the neck until you are dead and may God have mercy on your soul."[10] Without consulting with his local brethren, Upham set Amos's date of execution as June 28, 1805. The date gave county officials less than two weeks to construct the gallows.

Amos Babcock was led from the courthouse a condemned man. Peck's fallacious augury hailing the End of Days had at last proven correct, at least as far as Amos Babcock was concerned. As the final entry in a long string of morbid firsts, Amos Babcock would be the first to hang in Westmorland County.

Mortal Coils

John ✝ Jerome [1]

The name of Amos Babcock's executioner has never been disclosed, yet an understanding of the practices of the times coupled with deductive reasoning reveals the hangman's identity. Traditions in the British judiciary, the basis for the nascent Canadian legal system, held that a prisoner charged with a lesser crime be granted leniency in his own sentence in exchange for his services as executioner.[2] From the time of Amos's arrest in February through his execution, only one other prisoner was detained in the Dorchester jail: the indicted burglar and horse thief John Jerome.

Jerome was among the rogues' gallery of faceless, nameless, landless, lawless delinquents who gravitated toward the larger settlements of the new frontier. They came in search of short work, easy money, and vices hard to come by in the rural countryside. John Jerome was an illiterate labourer, roughly twenty-five years of age, with a sharp tendency toward mischief when intoxicated. His most recent crime spree had begun at 11:00 p.m. on the night of February 7, 1805. While well in his cups, Jerome "stole a horse from a Frenchman,"[3] which he then rode to the house of a local gentleman, Mr. James Law, Esquire. Upon breaking and entering the home, Jerome proceeded to steal one waistcoat, one-half silk handkerchief, a pair of men's shoes, and a razor case. What he intended to do with this motley sartorial collection remained a mystery to Jerome, even after he sobered up. Clutching his ill-gotten booty, Jerome remounted his stolen horse and rode to the home of his acquaintance, William Wellington, where he hid the loot and promptly passed out.[4] James Law, awakened during the drunken ransacking of his home, did not hesitate to press charges the following morning, and at Law's insistence, Jerome was quickly arrested. Brought before Westmorland Justice Samuel Gay, Jerome confessed he "was in his liquor" at the time of the offence and had fully intended to return the stolen goods once sober.[5] Gay was unmoved by the labourer's tale, and Jerome was indicted for burglary on February 9.

Jerome, unable to raise the modest £10 bail, languished in the dungeon, tortured by the sounds of drunken revelry resonating from the tavern above his head. One week later, Jerome's misery found company when he was forced to share his cell and irons with the abstemious and borderline lunatic Amos Babcock. What, if anything, the two men talked about during their lengthy incarceration remains a matter of speculation. They had little in common. Babcock was more than twice Jerome's age. Jerome was single and childless, the antithesis of Babcock's familial existence. There is nothing in his history to suggest Jerome held any strong religious beliefs, much less shared Babcock's ardent zeal. How these two disparate souls wiled away the weeks and months spent chained together — alone in a dank dungeon, with only the occasional interruption by their often-intoxicated jailer, Robert Keillor, as their lone source of distraction — staggers the imagination.

The fates of Westmorland's entire prison population would soon be joined by more than mere leg irons. Judge Joshua Upham, knowing the likely outcome of Babcock's trial, recognized the impending need for an executioner. His options were John Jerome or Jacob Peck. The irony of having Peck serve as Babcock's hangman was simply too great, even for the prosaic magistrate. That left Jerome. The indefinite postponement of Jerome's trial and the ambiguity of court records regarding his sentence suggest that a decision regarding Jerome's future role was made long before he was called to the bar. Based on his reaction in court, it is unlikely Jerome was told of his new profession until after he was returned to his cell. Under the "Bloody Code," more than two hundred and fifty offences, including the crime of burglary, were punishable by death. To escape the hangman's noose himself, Jerome had little choice but to agree to perform the deadly deed on his fellow inmate.

In the days following the guilty verdict, what remained of Amos's life shrunk to the dimensions of his dungeon cell. Jerome, on the other hand, was marshalled into action and found himself at liberty within the courthouse. Having agreed to carry out the execution in exchange for his freedom, Jerome now held a long list of preparations and little time to complete it. In the halcyon days of the early nineteenth century, the law mandated all executions be held in public view, a practice that continued unabated until 1868, when growing public outrage and rioting forced the government to perform the deadly spectacle quietly behind jailhouse walls.

Although no historical records specify the exact configuration of the first scaffold built at the Dorchester Courthouse, it likely conformed to the standards of the times. The "long drop" method, using a trap door and an extended fall to break the neck of the condemned, was not introduced until 1872. The scaffold that shepherded Amos Babcock to his much-desired afterlife was a far simpler affair, albeit a much less humane one. The ubiquitous "short drop" method meant a prolonged horrific death by strangulation rather than the instantaneous demise of a broken neck. Typically, the scaffold was little more than a nearby sturdy tree. The accused would be hoisted up on a ladder, put on horseback, or raised on the back of a wheeled cart and have a fixed-length rope tied around his neck. In his final moment, the support would be removed and the condemned was left to strangle slowly at the end of the rope.

For Amos Babcock, there would be no ceremonial last meal. The law of the land dictated that, "during the short but awful interval between sentence and execution, the prisoner shall be kept alone and sustained with only bread and water."[6] Under such meagre rations, Amos lost a great deal of weight. As the day of his execution dawned, he emerged a spectral figure, his clothes hanging upon him like those of a scarecrow. Moribund, he was already dead.

Thanks to Jerome's efforts, the execution took place as scheduled, in the pearl grey dawn of June 28, 1805. As he was led to the gallows, Amos's wrists were bound. Pinioning — another rope wrapped around the arms and torso at the elbows — allowed the prisoner to pray. As was customary, Amos was not fitted with a full hood but was mercifully blindfolded once on the scaffold. What bore Amos to his noose — a ladder, cart, horse, or some other contraption — was not recorded.

It was widely reported that, when using the short drop method, the hangman often pulled on the legs of the condemned to increase pressure on the neck and hasten his demise. There is no direct evidence this occurred during Babcock's execution, although it remains a distinct possibility. No eyewitness accounts survive of the hanging itself. Having spent five months incarcerated with Babcock, it is difficult to surmise how Jerome felt about his cell mate on the day of his execution. Perhaps Jerome sympathized with the condemned man and afforded him some small mercy at the end. Maybe he hated Babcock and left him to twist.

Execution practices at the time contained no requirement that a doctor be present to pronounce death. Babcock was left to hang until all movement stopped and the last signs of life left him. At that point, the responsibility for cutting him down and disposing of the body fell to John Jerome and to Robert Keillor, as county jailer. In 1752 a law was introduced that prohibited the return of the bodies of executed murderers to their families for burial, the government arguing such men did not deserve to rest in consecrated ground. Typically, the executed were buried below the gallows where they were hanged. Such was the fate of Amos Babcock. He was buried in the small graveyard behind the courthouse, its first occupant. Digging the grave had topped Jerome's to-do list. Nothing marks Amos's final resting place. No family member mourned his passing. No ceremony was permitted, and the Babcocks could not have attended the burial even if they had wanted to. Nothing suggests they had.

Act 7
Justice Denied

A Discernible Shift

The hanging took place as scheduled. Thereafter,
there was strong feeling against Jacob Peck.
— John Clarence Webster, 1928[1]

In the wake of Amos Babcock's execution, a discernible shift in public sentiment took hold. Babcock's trial exposed the true extent of Peck's machinations. The fraudulent preacher and his so-called prophesies were the catalyst for Babcock's actions, causing many to rethink Peck's legal culpability in the killing of Mercy Hall. Chief among them was prosecutor Ward Chipman.

As the broadsheets hit the streets of Halifax and Saint John on June 26, 1805, their pages contained the first media accounts of the tale. The subtle shifting of blame from Babcock to Peck was evident in the *Royal Gazette* report on Amos's trial. The newly executed Babcock was mentioned only once in the article. The pressing question of Peck's involvement received far more play:

> It appeared in evidence that for some time before the murder was committed, the prisoner with several of his neighbours, had been in the habit of meeting under a pretense of religious exercises at each others houses, at which one *Jacob Peck* was a principle performer; that they were under strong delusion and conducted themselves in a very frantic, irregular and even impious manner, and that in consequence of some pretended prophesies by some of the company in their pre-

tended religious phrenzies against the unfortunate deceased; the prisoner was probably induced to commit the horrid, barbarous and cruel murder of which he was convicted.[2]

The article's scandalized and incendiary tone finds its proper context when the true author of the piece is considered. At the time, newspapers had few salaried reporters to dispatch across the territory to cover court proceedings, even ones as rare and noteworthy as murder trials. Accordingly, the practice of the day was for those directly involved in the case — typically the clerk of the court or the chief prosecutor — to summarize the trial and provide the local tabloids with a first-hand, albeit somewhat biased, account. Such was the case with the Babcock trial, as none other than Ward Chipman wrote the *Royal Gazette* dispatch.[3] Reading between the lines reveals the untenable position in which the prosecutor now found himself. Chipman had still to try Jacob Peck on the charges of sedition and blasphemy, despite now having evidence Peck was guilty of a far more serious offence. Chipman's revised agenda is made clear in the final passages of the article:

> The above named *Jacob Peck* was on the same day indicted for blasphemous, prophane [*Sic*] and seditious language at the meetings above-mentioned, and recognized with good sureties to appear at the next Court of Oyer and Terminer in that County, to prosecute his traverse to the said indictment with effect.
>
> It is hoped and expected that these legal proceedings will have a good effect in putting an end to the strange and lamentable delusion, which made them necessary, and brought the unhappy culprit to such an ignominious death.[4]

Chipman's hopes that Peck's impending trial would bring the matter to a satisfactory end were a tad naive and ultimately vanquished. The case of *The Crown v. Jacob Peck* met with neither a hasty nor satisfying conclusion, as history would soon reveal.

 Act 7 **Justice Denied**

A satisfactory end would also elude many of the key players in the sad saga of Amos Babcock. Following his very public execution, the surviving Babcocks struggled to right themselves and salvage what they could of their name and reputation. Infamy had replaced poverty as the family's cross to bear. Of her own accord, the family matriarch, Dorcas Bennett Babcock — who had testified fearlessly against her husband and whose words also had helped impugn the instigator, Jacob Peck — quietly evanesced from the public record. In the months after Amos swung, Dorcas kept the children sequestered in the house on the road to Cocagne, courtesy of the continued charity and goodwill of William Hanington. Like her husband, Dorcas was proud. She recognized trading on her landlord's good nature was not a permanent solution to her problems. Dorcas found herself trapped in the same unenviable position as all widows of her day: she had no marketable skills, no inheritance, and no source of income. Dorcas was too old and too notorious to hope to remarry. Amos's single devastating act had left her with few options. Even with her young sons, Dorcas could not maintain the farm without Amos. Except for the Haningtons, community support had dwindled, replaced with pity, recriminations, and even contempt. Marked with the stigmata of Amos's crime, the family had become social pariahs, evoking fear and disdain among their once hospitable neighbours.

For their final helping of ignominy, the spectre of Captain Gideon Palmer — gentleman and the Lord's own coroner — again reared its taxing head. The king now laid claim to the bulk of Babcock's pitiful estate — the entire £18 and change. Palmer's inventory of Babcock's worldly goods had reached the county's collectors, along with word of Amos's untimely demise. The Crown came to collect, stripping the family of any and all valuables save for some modest kitchenware and the clothes on their backs. The family's possessions — of the poorest quality when new and now a heart-rending farrago of homespun repairs — were carted away, destined for auction or, more likely, the rubbish heap.

Dorcas's fortitude, so evident on the witness stand, was sorely tested once again. She had four brothers — Caleb, John, Benjamin, and Nathan — all living in Hopewell Cape alongside their parents. Ever the pragmatist,

Dorcas reasoned if she was fated to rely on the kindness of others to survive, that kindness must come from her kin. She packed up the children and their last meagre belongings and headed south to Hopewell.

What became of Dorcas Babcock after that is lost to time. She never appeared in any subsequent New Brunswick census, nor was she mentioned in her father's will.[5] How and when she died escaped all notice. No tombstone marks where she now lies. In the end, she was nothing more than a widow in a place that had them to spare. In trying to live down the shame, she succeeded in rendering herself invisible.

The Babcocks' nine children, forever haunted by the terrifying memory of what they were forced to witness, slowly scattered throughout the Maritimes. Their eldest daughter Dorcas — the prophetess who had mouthed Peck's Doomsday message to such lethal effect — survived seventy-eight years. In her later days, she never spoke of her pivotal role in the events that claimed her aunt and her father. Henry and Caleb — the "Sons of Gideon" who valiantly rose to their father's aid — both secured land in Sackville, New Brunswick.[6] There, they married and lived out their days, cursed by the Babcock name.[7] The middle daughters — Anne, Mary, and Delilah — fared best. All found good husbands, settled throughout New Brunswick, and lived well into their seventies. Sarah, the daughter Amos choked and cast into the wall, later married William McGee. The couple made a home near Coverdale, where she died at the age of fifty-one. Her youngest sisters — Elizabeth and Amy — married the Sears brothers, William and Thomas. Both girls perished far too young, Elizabeth at forty-six,[8] Amy at forty-nine.

The infamy of the Babcock name also stained Amos's brother Jonathon, the key witness for the prosecution. Unlucky in the New Brunswick land lottery and facing relentless social stigma in Shediac Parish, Jonathon eventually admitted defeat. In 1808 he took his wife and three of his youngest children and returned to Nova Scotia. They settled near his wife's family in Canning. Jonathon lived out the remainder of his days in relative obscurity and penury, haunted by his inability to save his sister, his brother, or himself.[9]

The other key witness for the prosecution — William Hanington — fared far better, mercifully having no familial ties to the crime.[10] In the years following Babcock's trial, Hanington's various business ventures flourished, as did his family. His son, Daniel (1804-1889) became a prominent provincial politician and was eventually named speaker of the New Brunswick House of Assembly.

In 1831 William Hanington suffered a stroke from which he never fully recovered. He died seven years later, a mere shadow of the once great adventurer who first settled the now-bustling town of Shediac. He is buried in the cemetery of St. Martin's-in-the-Woods, a church he helped build in the wake of the Peck-Babcock debacle. He rests alongside his beloved formidable disobedient wife Mary.

As the *annus horribilis* of 1805 drew to a close, all the central figures in the Amos Babcock saga were present, accounted for, and trying to rebuild their shattered lives, save one. There was still the lingering issue of the vexatious preacher, Jacob Peck. As Ward Chipman so wistfully predicted, the community would not rest until Jacob Peck was brought to justice.

Hindsight

Jacob Peck[1]

There is nothing available to show what became of Jacob Peck.

— William Reynolds, 1898[2]

As for the chief perpetrator of these delusions, he seems to have disappeared from both the revivalist circuit and from history, and there's nothing to show that Jacob Peck ever came before earthly justice.

— B.J. Grant, 1983[3]

Having money at hand, Jacob paid bail and left prison. When his court date rolled around and he was to answer for the "very frantic, irregular and even impious manner" in which he held his revival meetings, he never showed up. Jacob Peck seems to have disappeared from the pages of history.

— Allison Finnamore, 2005[4]

The notion that Peck simply vanished after his brief court appearance in 1805 is as erroneous as it is ubiquitous. If Peck went into hiding, he did so in plain sight and with brazen indifference. Contrary to popular belief, Peck attended the first two of his scheduled court appearances and possibly more. At the start of his legal troubles, he was consistently compliant.

After his arrest warrant was issued on February 22, 1805, Peck presented himself to the court three days later, at which time he posted bail. Peck then returned to court on June 15 as scheduled, at which time his hearing was postponed due to mysterious missing witnesses. After posting a second bond, he was instructed to return at the next general session.

In the meantime, Peck returned to his life in Salisbury Parish and did little to maintain a low profile. In 1806 he married Ann Horsman in a ceremony certified by Justice William Sinton, Esquire.[5] In an ironic twist, he also resumed his duties as constable for Salisbury Parish through the end of 1805 and was entrusted with maintaining law and order in the district.[6] Following that, Peck took up a series of appointed positions in the parish, including a stint as Observer of the Poor in 1807-1808, and the equally lowly post of Observer of Fences in 1809. He distinguished himself in neither capacity. The activities of such positions, particularly those relating to the indigent, were faithfully documented in the Public Records of Westmorland County. Appointees were expected to make regular reports of their endeavours, yet, for the periods in which Peck served, the records are conspicuously quiet. Whether this was on account of his illiteracy or his indifference cannot be discerned.

With all due respect to past chroniclers of this tale, Jacob Peck did not vanish from history so much as history itself disappeared.[7] Court records from the crucial period are missing, perhaps destroyed by flood or fire or lost to negligence and the ravages of time. Misperceptions as to the deposition of the case originate not from Peck's wanton behaviour but from an irreparable hole in an already skeletal public record. Though the idea of Peck's refusing to appear is both dramatically satisfying and entirely consistent with his character, the surviving documents indicate Peck did comply with the court's instructions, with one small but telling exception.

Deep in the recesses of the New Brunswick Museum Archives an ordinary note sits idle in an accounting file for the clerk of the Crown on the circuits from the county of Westmorland dating from June 1809. At the end of a lengthy recitation of various bits of governmental fiscal exchange, a single entry states that in the matter of *The King versus Jacob*

Peck, the accused forfeited his bond.[8] As such, the Crown was entitled to retain the £100 lawful money Peck had paid to secure his freedom. The note, a mere clerical accounting, gives no reason for the forfeiture, although bonds typically were revoked for failing to appear as commanded. The note gives no indication whether Peck's most recent sureties — preacher Henry Steeves and the mysterious Daniel McDonald — were required to forfeit their bonds as well.

Two key points can be inferred from the note: first, that Peck's legal troubles continued for several years after Babcock's execution — at least through the summer of 1809; and second, that Peck failed to appear as scheduled on at least one occasion. Aside from this lone cryptic reference, court records on the matter of the unrepentant cleric are no more.

Although David Graham Bell contends that the authorities of Westmorland opted not to proceed with Peck's trial on blasphemy and sedition charges because they "thought it best to let the whole Babcock affair rest,"[9] the accounting note reveals that the matter was not entirely dropped. It appears the case languished for years, repeatedly carried over or postponed, suggesting the court was not quite ready to let it rest. Furthermore, the source of the delay was not Peck but the presiding judge, the Honourable Joshua Upham.

The trial completed, Judge Upham beat a hasty retreat from Dorchester. He was glad to see the back of it. The once-dignified confines of the court had been reduced to a common tavern, full of ill-informed opinions and armchair jurists. He returned to his comfortable home in French Village, fated never again to endure the hardships of life on the *nisi prius* circuit.

The end of Upham's circuit days did not come by choice. In the months following the trial, Upham continued his diatribes against the shameful conditions of the roads and, more important, his crusade for greater recognition and higher wages for the judges of the Supreme Court. In a last-ditch effort — and with flagrant disregard for his arthritis, age, and failing health — Upham made a final extraordinary plea and one last arduous voyage.[10] In the summer of 1807, he travelled by canoe from his home to Saint John, where he then made passage to England. Driven by an ardour that silenced his discomfort, his singular mission was to petition for an increase in salary on behalf of all the sitting Supreme Court justices. In a cautious yet forcefully worded proposal, Upham and his fellows demanded a raise, from £300 to £500 per year for puisne judges and from £500 to £700 for the chief justice.

After a debilitating journey, Upham at last set foot in England, spoiling for a fight. When he was finally granted an audience with his superiors, he opened his address by plangently declaring he would not leave until his demands were met. Whether to silence this most vocal supplicant or as a tacit acknowledgment that the raise was past due, the British government ceded to his request. Triumphant, Upham booked his return passage to Saint John. In a last cruel twist of fate, the judge would not live to reap the benefits of his impassioned plea. He died on November 1, 1808, in Saint John, shortly after his ship docked in port.

His wife Mary took up the fight, though likely more out of necessity than remembrance. On June 9, 1809, she petitioned the British government to have Upham's salary increase given to her and "a large family of children, many of them very young, without any means of support."[11] After much debate and careful consideration, the British granted her petition, awarding her a one-time payment of £200, with a further £100 granted to the couple's eldest daughter, Elizabeth. The money did not last long, and Mary Upham died in 1826, virtually penniless.

Upham's odyssey and untimely death disrupted the *nisi prius* circuit schedule for years. All cases in the affected jurisdictions, including Westmorland, were postponed until further notice. Joshua Upham's sudden demise on the Saint John dock also left a void on the bench of the Supreme Court. After a suitable period of mourning, in which all contenders for the job subtly jockeyed for position, Upham's seat on the bench was at last filled by none other than the Solicitor General, Ward Chipman Sr.[12] Chipman's ascension to the highest court in the province was a boon for jurisprudence in New Brunswick but proved a bust in the matter of Jacob Peck. Because Chipman had served as chief prosecutor in the case, he was forced to recuse himself as presiding judge, causing further delays and much legal hand wringing. By the summer of 1809, Chipman was firmly installed on the bench and had assumed Upham's duties on the *nisi prius* circuit, but his recusal meant the docket for the summer session in Westmorland could not include the case against Jacob Peck. Standard procedure would have seen the case transferred to another jurisdiction, but no record of such a transfer survives.

The promotion of Ward Chipman to the Supreme Court coincided with another relevant development: the loss of Westmorland's clerk of the court, Hezekiah King. Both King and Chipman were dogged recordkeepers, and it was largely due to their efforts that so much of the documentation relating to Peck and Babcock survives. With King gone and Chipman now clad in the finest robes, recordkeeping at the Dorchester Courthouse took a decided turn for the worse. It was at this stage that the court's archival record fell silent. It would not resume until 1818, by which time Peck was dead or the case had been resolved or forgotten.

Fortunately, court documents are not our ancestors' only legacy. The last unambiguous trace of Peck in the historical record comes on July 24, 1810, when the one-time preacher had the unmitigated gall to petition yet again for free land from the county and Crown that had spent the past five years prosecuting him for treason.[13] At the time of his petition, Peck had taken up residence on a tract of land in Salisbury along the Petitcodiac River. The land originally had been granted to Martin Gay, Esquire. Peck and his fellow petitioners requested the land adjacent to their current home, "which would prevent many disturbing stances and a number of expensive lawsuits and...enable us to sit in peace."[14] Although a number of applicants were awarded land, Peck was not. His petition was denied not because of his seditious behaviour but because the land, in fact, was not vacant, having already been allocated by a faulty prior survey. At least, that is what the Crown's rejection letter claimed.[15]

There remains one last possible hint of Jacob Peck in the public record. The year is 1823, the month and day are not specified. On a small scrap of paper housed in the Provincial Archives of New Brunswick is a handwritten notation from the clerk of the Supreme Court.[16] A man by the name of Christian Steeves had filed a lawsuit against a Jacob Peck of unknown address. The note stipulates only that Peck, having been served with notice of the suit, was delivered to bail. There is no mention of the basis of the suit, and we cannot be sure if the defendant in the case is indeed our Jacob Peck. The possibility is lent credence by the fact that Christian Steeves lived in Hillsborough at the same time as Peck and there was a long-standing relationship between Jacob and the Steeves family.[17] Whatever the grievance, the lawsuit appears to have been dropped. There is no record regarding the disposition of the case in any existing court documents. If it was the same Jacob Peck, he would have been fifty-eight years old.

Though past renditions of the ballad of Jacob Peck are plagued by error and speculative imaginings, they are correct on one key point: what ultimately became of Jacob Peck remains a mystery. His death predated all formal social tracking in the region, and no death certificate, church record, gravestone, or probate record marks his passing.

In all probability, his mortal remains lie in the Burnt Hills Burial Ground near Salisbury Parish.[18] No reliquary bears notice to his final resting place. Often referred to as the Thaney Smith Cemetery, the graveyard is situated on the right bank of the Pollett River. Jacob's younger brother Leonard is buried there, immortalized by a simple stone that bears his date of death — January 4, 1822 — at the age of forty-seven. Ill-positioned on a chronic flood plain, the cemetery was submerged repeatedly and eventually abandoned. Time and neglect have caused it to fall into disrepair, and the majority of the gravestones have been lost.[19]

Peck's self-fabricated legend has been obscured by time, poverty, a lack of acknowledged descendants, and more than a little purposeful deception. He undoubtedly died as he had lived, surrounded by his own web of delusion, grandiosity, and bathos. Yet, for all the feckless preacher's posturing and pomposity, he did not enter the annals of history of his own accord. Were it not for the actions of another — the humble crofter Amos Babcock — Jacob Peck would have remained as inconsequential and overlooked in death as he was in life.

Postscript
Quaeitur

The crime of solicitation is "over with the asking." Once the solicitor encourages, promotes, or advocates an illegal act, the violation is complete. The tangible consequences of the incitement are technically irrelevant. In the case at hand, history records those most tangible consequences: Jacob Peck incited, Amos Babcock acted, Mercy Hall died.

What history also records is that in the death of Mercy Hall, justice has been denied for more than two centuries. In addition to the crimes for which he was formally indicted, blasphemy and sedition, I contend Jacob Peck should have been charged with a far more serious offence — namely, solicitation of murder. This account has served, for all intents and purposes, as the prosecution's case against Jacob Peck on all three counts.

Within these pages, Jacob Peck has received no defence. He is no more entitled to one now than he was in 1805. Peck remains "innocent until proven guilty," even though that phrase, coined by British barrister Sir William Garrow, did not enter into common usage until the decade following Babcock's execution.[1]

It now falls to you, reader as juror, to sit in judgment. As with any trial, before you deliberate there are instructions you must receive, guidelines you must follow, and additional issues to consider before rendering a verdict.

First, you must free yourself of your own misperceptions regarding legal procedure. The sad truth is that most Canadians derive their knowledge of the law from American entertainment. As a result, our understanding of trial procedures is often flawed, not only because of liberties taken by producers to advance plot lines but also because of fundamental differences in legal procedure across the border. In this particular instance, the problem is further compounded because the standards applied must be those in force in 1805. Mercifully, our legal system has matured and evolved in the intervening centuries, even if we are largely unaware of the changes. Case in point: under current Canadian law, Peck's offence is now known as "counselling," as defined in section 464(a) of the Criminal Code. The change was intended to differentiate generalized incitement of crime from acts specific to prostitution. Semantics aside, in 1805, as now, it was and remains a criminal offence to make statements that promote, incite, or encourage the commission of an illegal act. Although now most often invoked in cases of murder for hire, the crime has been applied to the incitement of genocide[2] and to propaganda promoting hate crimes.[3]

Our media-derived misperceptions also extend to the backbone of the judicial system: the forensic sciences. Without question, our technological capacity in criminal investigations has grown in the intervening years, although sometimes at a much slower rate than television crime dramas would have you believe. Thanks to what has been dubbed the "CSI Effect," audiences and jurors alike have come to expect a high-tech solution to every crime. Yet, for all our advances in forensic science, DNA testing and blood spatter analysis can contribute nothing toward our understanding of who was responsible for the murder of Mercy Hall. The question of Peck's guilt or innocence cannot be resolved by analyzing physical evidence; the assessment relies solely on the interpretation of his behaviour and what that behaviour reveals about his intent. The case is about societal standards of conduct and personal responsibility, not fingerprints. In that regard, time and technology have stood still. The witness statements and personal correspondence sit preserved in the archives, exactly as they were in 1805.

Postscript Quaeitur

Second, and along the same lines, is the issue of motive. The emphasis placed on establishing a motive in criminal trials is also an artifact of fictionalized courtroom dramas. Yet, despite the current fascination with motive in the popular media, legally it is often meaningless. Once the prosecution has shown that the accused acted with intent, the necessary elements of the crime have been established and the jury is instructed to render its verdict accordingly.

Our modern obsession with motive reflects human nature, not legal necessity. We want to know why the accused committed the heinous act. As the judicial system advanced, lawyers quickly learned that juries were hesitant to convict if they could not understand the perpetrator's reasons for the crime, especially in cases of murder. Even if it is not legally mandated, motive is emotionally required. It helps to rationalize an irrational act.

So what of Amos and Mercy and Jacob? Once the prosecution established the killing had not been done in self-defence, it was legally immaterial why Amos killed his sister. That he believed he was acting under orders from God did not render the act lawful any more than if he had done it out of greed or anger. By the same token, identifying a specific motive for the actions of Jacob Peck is not required in order to establish his criminal culpability. The preacher could have ordered the sacrifice of Mercy for any number of reasons. Peck was likely testing the level of control he had over Babcock. Perhaps Peck's motive was to test the limits of the benefits of clergy, particularly as it applied to Europeans from the lower classes. As the Mosley case attests, invoking *w* saved a female slave from the gallows. Peck might have used Babcock to test the court, either as a safeguard for some past crime or as a hedge against some future offence. If Amos Babcock was Jacob Peck's experiment in arcane law, Babcock proved an apt test subject as Peck had no more formal status as clergy than Babcock. Indeed, if this was the preacher's aim, the experiment was a success for Peck, even as it proved a lethal failure for Babcock.

Perhaps Peck's rationale was more personal, something specific to Mercy herself. Had Peck lusted after Mercy and been rebuffed? Perhaps she insulted his inflated sense of self and the preacher used Amos to retaliate. It could be that Mercy saw through Peck's machinations and he wanted her silenced. And maybe we are trying too hard to find a reason where none existed. When it comes to the motivations of con men and narcissists, history has shown that self-aggrandizement and the protection of carefully crafted facades are principle driving forces. To look for rationales beyond that might be to give Peck too much credit. Regardless, the potential motives are many but the outcome remains the same. To reach a guilty verdict, you do not need to know why Peck solicited Amos; you need only believe that he did solicit him.

Third, and perhaps most significantly, we must look at how the crime of solicitation is defined and applied. To start, it is imperative that Peck be held to a lesser standard than Amos. One reason inchoate crimes such as incitement remain controversial is that the burden of proof is lower than for other capital offences, particularly regarding the accused's state of mind. The prosecution is not required to prove that Jacob Peck intended to kill Mercy Hall. Rather, the Crown needs only show that Peck meant to influence or manipulate Amos Babcock. Babcock's subsequent actions alone provide the evidence necessary to satisfy the lesser burden.

Nor does the crime require Peck to have directly told Amos to kill. That Peck used Babcock's own daughter to convey his fatalistic message renders the deed more heinous and cold-blooded but in no way reduces Peck's culpability. Further, the law does not demand that Amos comply with Peck's commands, although events show that, tragically, he did. To find Peck guilty, you need believe only that the self-declared evangelist's actions were purposeful and voluntary. Alternatively, you may find that he acted with complete criminal recklessness — that Peck sent forth his deadly message with utter disregard for the consequences. In either case, the conclusion is the same: Peck is guilty of the crime of inciting the murder of Mercy Hall.

In considering the issue of intent, recall the specifics of the revival of February 12. Despite the diverse crowd of followers assembled, it is clear Peck's message was not intended for all. It was specific to Amos Babcock. Peck manipulated Babcock's eldest daughter to play on Amos's emotions and his unwavering religious convictions. The preacher painted a dire picture: Judgment Day was at hand. The end of the world was to be that very night. In order to save himself, his wife, and his children, Peck led Babcock to believe he had only one option, a last ray of hope: his sister, Mercy. According to Peck, Mercy was destined to perish. She would not survive the coming apocalypse. Yet, through her death, she would provide redemption for Amos and his offspring. In Babcock's deluded state, in his desperation for eternal salvation, Peck's words convinced Amos he had no choice but to ensure his sister's death so that he and his kin would be Raptured.

Given the legal parameters of solicitation, it is immaterial whether Peck intended this apocryphal tale as a blueprint for murder or merely as a parable to shock its recipient into submission. What matters, under the law, is that Peck intended to manipulate and control Amos's emotions and to incite him to action. The outcome of that incitement was murder. Jacob Peck's sermon encouraged the crime, making Jacob Peck legally responsible for its commission. The preacher's choice of words was not merely ill-conceived or unfortunate; it rose to the level of criminal.

Peck's reckless disregard for the consequences of his actions arose from his own malignant hall of mirrors. Peck sought only his own power and glory. That single-minded quest coupled with his chronic lack of empathy rendered Amos Babcock invisible. Peck quite literally did not care what Amos did, so long as Amos's devotion to Peck remained intact. Mercy's death was the result of indifference, if not actual intent.

At its heart, this case is little more than the lamentable meeting of two delusional men, each trapped in a fantasy world of his own design. Jacob Peck, damned at birth to a life of penury and obscurity, retreated into a chrysalis of deceit, magical thinking, and nihilism. In a fever of self-reinvention, he emerged as a gentleman scholar and paragon of piety, modelling himself after the true men of God who stoked his envy: Henry Steeves and Joseph Crandall. Peck's illusions of grandeur — claiming nothing short of sharing private correspondence with the king and of being Christ's own redeemer — and his false promise of salvation were the fertile ground in which Amos Babcock's hallucinations took root.

Babcock, disillusioned and battered in this world, put his faith in God to provide in the next.

As the reality of Babcock's world grew bleaker and harder to bear, the facade that was Jacob Peck arrived in Shediac at the right time with the right message. Having recognized the other as kindred, Babcock's and Peck's twin delusions meshed, fed upon each other, and swelled, obliterating all reason: two men, deluded, unstable, and driven by demons they could neither name nor acknowledge. United in fantasy and ruinous fanaticism, they were mutually responsible for the death of Mercy Hall, co-conspirators in a plot conceived by Peck and executed by Babcock. To date, Amos Babcock alone has paid the price for their sins.

Finding Jacob Peck culpable does not absolve Amos Babcock of guilt in the crime. Babcock held the knife that killed Mercy and, as such, remains accountable for his own actions. The only thing that could have saved Amos was the one option he never considered: a plea of not guilty by reason of insanity.

Although times and laws have changed, when it comes to the question of sanity the century in which the crime was committed is of no relevance. As Marilyn Pilon notes: "Canadian criminal code has always provided that persons will not be held criminally liable for their actions if their mental state at the time rendered them 'incapable of appreciating' the nature and quality of the act and knowing that it was wrong."[4]

If you are convinced Amos Babcock is not guilty by reason of insanity, you are not alone. In 1898 William K. Reynolds wrote: "That a crazy man should be arraigned, tried and condemned without counsel for his defense seems incredible in the light of modern jurisprudence, as does the fact that he was hanged for a crime for which he was not morally responsible. In these days such a man would be sent to an asylum for the insane."[5] In the same vein, in 1915 Joseph W. Lawrence suggested that:

> [c]ontrasting this case with cases of the same nature occur-
> ring in modern times, the most striking feature . . . is the
> apparent absence of any attempt to contend that Babcock
> was not responsible for his hideous act . . . there can scarcely

be a question that no tribunal of to-day would hold one in Babcock's position guilty of murder, or would be justified in so doing.[6]

Any doubt regarding Babcock's sanity is now moot; his hanging made it so. But the question remains whether the itinerant preacher, Jacob Peck, was also responsible for the murder of Mercy Hall. History does not record him as such. A finding of guilt now is legally meaningless, yet the possibility of a moral victory remains, some small measure of justice for Mercy: the recognition of Peck's culpability in her murder, an acknowledgement of the wrongness of his actions, a long-evaded final day of reckoning for Jacob Peck.

As you ponder the issue — as you deliberate Peck's fate — the final determination of guilt or innocence lies in your answer to a single question: had Jacob Peck never travelled to Shediac Parish and the two men had never met, would Amos Babcock have killed his sister, Mercy Hall?

Acknowledgements

Trawling through the historic record can be an exasperating endeavour, but in this case it was one made easier by the exceptional curatorial staffs at the New Brunswick Museum Archives, the Provincial Archives of New Brunswick, and the Nova Scotia Archives. I am eternally grateful for their assistance. Thanks also to the librarians of the reference desks at the Central Branch of the Saint John Free Public Library, the Spring Garden branch of the Halifax Public Libraries, and the Loyalist Collection at the Harriet Irving Library at the University of New Brunswick.

Special thanks are due to David Mawhinney, Archivist of the Mount Allison University Archives, for all his efforts. I also offer heartfelt thanks to Dorothy, Ken, and Sandy at the Annapolis Royal Branch of the Annapolis Valley Regional Library for their endless patience, unwavering good humour, and functioning computers.

Aside from the major public archives, the regional museums and historical societies of the Maritimes are a treasure trove of riches. I am indebted to the Keillor House Museum, particularly its crack researcher Teresa Simpson, and to the Albert County Museum. A special place in my heart is also reserved for Eugene Goodrich, past president of the Westmorland Historical Society. Gene has an encyclopedic knowledge of the people and places at the heart of this particular tale, and it is comforting to know Canada's past is safe in the hands of such stewards. Finally, I am grateful to Heather Chevalier, a descendant of Amos Babcock, for forwarding her thoughts on the case and providing clues to her family's genealogy.

This book would not exist were it not for the eponymous song by John Bottomley. I was inspired to learn more about the saga after hearing John's powerful work. His death was a devastating loss to the Canadian music scene. I am so grateful to Angela Muellers, the executor of John's estate, for granting permission to have his lyrics introduce this book. Thanks are also due to David Basskin and Jordan Orava at CMRRA; Bogoreh Bogoreh at SOCAN; Tina Lusignan at the Copyright Board of Canada; and Sophie Givernaud at SODRAC for taking the time to answer my many emails and questions regarding the reprinting of lyrics.

It has been a pleasure and honour working with the good people at Goose Lane. They have made this experience one of the best of my professional career. Thanks to Susanne Alexander, Julie Scriver, James Duplacey, Colleen Kitts, Corey Redekop and Chris Tompkins for their patience, support, and guiding hands. I am also very grateful to Barry Norris, Paula Sarson and Dr. Megan Woodworth for their work on the manuscript.

Finally, none of this would have been possible without the tireless efforts of the folks at the Carolyn Swayze Agency, especially Carolyn and Kris. Thank you for the kind words, frank critiques, and the leaps of faith that have brought us this far.

Notes

Unless otherwise specified, all birth and death dates are drawn from parish and cemetery records or headstones. Marriage dates are taken from county registries, parish records, or bonds. The locations of residences are derived from census reports, land registries, deeds, or leases.

Preface: *In Limine*

1. Although Joseph Lawrence's paper was not published, its presentation is documented in the records of the New Brunswick Historical Society Fonds, New Brunswick Museum Archives [hereafter NBMA], S25-29 F1-303.
2. David Graham Bell first began mapping the origins of the Babcock tragedy in the popular record in *Newlight Baptist Journals of James Manning and James Innis* (Saint John, NB: Acadia Divinity College and the Baptist Historical Committee, 1984), appendix X.
3. The curious can find Paul Kimball's unique take on the Babcock saga at http://redstarfilms.blogspot.ca/2006/04/amos-babcock-crazed-murderer-or.html.

Prologue

1. The disposal of Mercy's body is related by William Hanington, letter to William Black, February 14, 1805, NBMA, Government Collection, S181 F107.5.
2. Reynolds wrote that Babcock had walked backwards toward the house, sweeping the snow with a broom as he went, yet there is no evidence to support the notion that Amos carried a broom as well as his sister's body, nor that he walked backwards after he disposed of her body; see William

Reynolds ["Roslynde," pseud.], "The Babcock Tragedy," *New Brunswick Magazine* (July 1898) p. 220.

The Arrival

1. This signature, attributed to Jacob Peck, was taken from his 1791 petition for land, Provincial Archives of New Brunswick [hereafter, PANB], F1038.
2. "Potquodiach" — William Hanington, letter to Amos Botsford, February 21, 1805, NBMA, Government Collection, S181 F107.7.
3. William Hanington's observations of Jacob Peck, which served as the basis of his eventual indictment on charges of blasphemy and sedition, were evident in several of Hanington's witness statements; NBMA, Government Collection, S181 F109.
4. Peck's affiliation with Henry Alline and the New Light movement was confirmed in a statement by John Welling, recounted in John Clarence Webster, *A History of Shediac, New Brunswick* (privately printed, 1928; reprinted Saint John, NB: New Brunswick Museum, 1953), p. 15.
5. "frolicking" — Greg Gordon, "Henry Alline — the Apostle of Nova Scotia," *Revival Preachers Circular*, no. 5.
6. "the Apostle of Nova Scotia," ibid.
7. Statistics on the French population are from the 1800-1804 census of Shediac (then called Jedaique by the Acadians) by the Mission of Saint Antoine of Richibucto; the estimate of English settlers is from the 1803 census.
8. Shediac would not build its first church until 1822, when St.-Martin's-in-the-Woods was constructed, as noted in Webster, *History of Shediac*.

Another Awakening

1. This signature and Jacob's mark are from the 1804 marriage bond of Jacob Peck and Joyce Alrod, NBMA, S89-2 F57.65.
2. The story of *The Pearl,* complete with passenger manifests, was provided by the Palatine Project, www.progenealogists.com/palproject.
3. Martin Peck and family (including young Jacob) are recorded in the 1770 census of Nova Scotia as living in Cumberland County; the census also clearly denotes their religious affiliation as Protestant.
4. Information relating to Nova Scotia land grants, including those of Martin Peck, Jonathon Babcock Sr., and Caleb Bennett, is retained at the Provincial Crown Lands Record Centre, Nova Scotia Department of National Resources, and the Crown Land Information Management Centre, both located in Halifax.
5. For Martin Peck's 1786 land grant, see PANB, F16302.
6. For Martin Peck's 1789 land grant, see ibid., F16300.
7. The judgments against Martin Peck are noted in the Westmorland Public Records, 1751-1883, Harriet Irving Library, C3201.

8. "a young man without family, no account of stock or grain" — from the Petition for the Regranting of the Hillsborough Land Grants, Joseph Gray, 1783, Fort Beauséjour-Fort Cumberland National Historic Site, Manuscript Collection.

9. For Jacob's 1791 petition for a land grant, see PANB, F1038.

10. "about Twenty years of age," ibid.

11. An entertaining and informative summary of parish governmental structure and the role of appointed officers can be found in W. Eugene Goodrich, "The Keillors of Keillor House: A Guide for Guides" (Dorchester, NB: Keillor House Museum, May 2011).

12. "being guilty of any neglect or misbehaviour" — Act for the Appointment of Town and Parish Officers in the Several Counties of this Province, S.N.B. 26 Geo III (1786) c. 28.

13. For an annual chronicle of Jacob and Martin's appointments to various parish posts, see General Records for Westmorland County, Harriet Irving Library, LPR.N4P8W4L6.

14. "another revivalist" — Reynolds, "Babcock Tragedy," p. 217.

15. "lurid declamations," ibid.

16. Peck's relationships with Steeves and Crandall were independently documented. Steeves agreed to serve as Peck's surety during the trial and Crandall was a co-petitioner with Peck in a land grant application in 1810, PANB, F4174.

17. For Peck's 1804 marriage bond, see NBMA, S89-2 F57.65.

18. For the 1806 marriage of Peck and Horsman, see the marriage registry for Westmorland County, Harriet Irving Library, LPR.N4C6S4W4M3R4.

19. "sum of Five Hundred Pounds" — Peck's 1804 marriage bond, NBMA, S89-2 F57.65.

20. For a notation indicating Neke Ayers was granted a licence to operate a tavern, see General Records of Westmorland County, Harriet Irving Library, LPR.N4P8W4L6.

21. Those interested in comparing Peck's signatures will find his third and final signature at the top of Chapter Thirty-two; Leonard Peck's signature appears at the top of Chapter Twenty-two.

The Mark

1. This putative signature of Amos Babcock comes from his 1803 petition for a land grant, PANB, F1043. The veracity of the signature is questionable. The text of the petition was written in a practised hand, the signatures are clearly by a different hand than the text, and all eleven signatures were written by the same person. Although it is possible Amos signed for the ten other applicants, it is more likely that one of the other applicants — perhaps one of the Killams, who were far more educated and known to be literate — signed on behalf of all petitioners. It remains,

however, the only surviving signature attributable to Amos Babcock in the historical record.

2. Details of the Babcock family genealogy initially came from an account by his paternal great-great-granddaughter, Heather Babcock Chevalier, of Moncton, New Brunswick, in 2009; all birth and death dates as well as the dates and locations of marriages were then confirmed by parish records and grave markers throughout Nova Scotia and New Brunswick.

3. Although Amos's birth predates the issuance of birth or christening certificates, other official documentation, including his marriage registration and multiple land grant petitions, confirm that his full and proper name was Amos Babcock.

4. For Jonathon Babcock's 1798 land grant application, see PANB, F1040.

5. For the land grant petition of Amos and Jonathon Babcock, see ibid., F1043.

6. "hard-working men, of little education" — Reynolds, "Babcock Tragedy," p. 216.

7. Biographic details of William Hanington, Hanington Family Fonds, NBMA, 0.5 CB DOC.1.

8. "Comely young woman" — Webster, *History of Shediac*, p. 8.

9. "it was a desperate case of first-sight affection," ibid.

10. The rental arrangement between Babcock and Hanington is described in Reynolds, "Babcock Tragedy"; and in Joseph W. Lawrence, *The Judges of New Brunswick and Their Times*, ed. A.A. Stockton and W.O. Raymond (Saint John, NB: Miramichi Books, 1915). Confirmation of the story comes from the mortgage deed between Casey and Atkinson, dated 1803, NBMA, Government Collection, S180 F48.8.

Collateral

1. "Concerning the victim" — Bell, *Newlight Baptist Journals*, p. 337.

2. Abner Hall's 1782 land purchase is documented in Nova Scotia Archives [hereafter, NSA], MFM 12261, Cornwallis Township Records, book C6, p. 46.

3. The birth dates of Mercy's eight children are recorded in the Cornwallis Township Book, microfilm, NSA, MFM 15031.

4. Sadly, Dorcas Babcock's feelings about her sister-in-law, contained in her witness statement before the grand jury, have been lost. The statement appears to be among the sources referenced by Reynolds, "Babcock Tragedy." Clues to its content, however, can be gleaned from notes made by Ward Chipman, Library and Archives Canada [hereafter, LAC], R5176-0-0-E, 65.

5. "reprobate" — Ward Chipman's draft of his opening remarks, also reprinted in a redacted form in Bell, *Newlight Baptist Journals*, p. 344.

6. "ignominious" — from an account of the trial in the *Royal Gazette*, June 26, 1805.
7. "melancholy disposition" and "not allowed to eat with the others of the family" — Reynolds, "Babcock Tragedy," p. 216.
8. "quite right in the head" — B.J. Grant, *Six for the Hangman* (Fredericton, NB: Fiddlehead Poetry Books and Goose Lane Editions, 1983), p. 95.

Best Laid Plans
1. Hanington's ornate signature is from the bail bond he signed as a surety for Jonathon Babcock on March 6, 1805, NBMA, S181 F107.2. Hanington's signature on other unrelated documents typically is far more decorative and elaborate, occasionally bordering on the ridiculous.
2. Biographical details of Hanington's early life are from Hanington Family Fonds, NBMA, 0.5 CB DOC 1.
3. Hanington's land swap with Williams and his trek to Halifax in search of a frying pan are recounted in Fannie Chandler Bell, *A History of Old Shediac, New Brunswick* (Moncton, NB: National Print, 1937).
4. The story of the beaver pelt and the details of Hanington's store are from Webster, *History of Shediac*, pp. 9-10; notes relating to William Hanington are in NBMA, William Lusk Webster Collection, 24-1 F6-3.

Vicious Propensity
1. "The melancholy affair" — Hanington, letter to Botsford, February 21, 1805, NBMA, S181 F107.7.
2. Hanington documented Peck's activities in three documents: ibid.; letter to William Black, February 14, 1805, NBMA, S181 F107.5; and his transcript of the revival, forwarded to the Justices of Westmorland, NBMA, S181 F107.6. Although he did not attend many of the revivals himself, he "was credibly informed" of the goings-on by his wife, Mary.
3. "they were alarmed by a great noise" — Hanington, letter to Botsford, February 21, 1805, NBMA, S181 F107.7.
4. "Jacob Peck supported Amos Babcock in everything he said or did" — ibid.

Neglect and Regret
1. The story of Babcock's neglect of the cattle and his confrontation by Hanington is reported in Reynolds, "Babcock Tragedy," p. 218; and in Lawrence, *Judges of New Brunswick*, p. 87. The incident was presumably taken from a now-absent witness statement of William Hanington's to which Reynolds and/or Lawrence had access in the 1800s. Attempts to verify independently the account in the extant historic record proved fruitless, beyond confirming that Hanington raised cattle and the location of Poirier's house relative to the barn near Babcock's home.

2. "the Lord will provide" — quoted in Lawrence, *Judges of New Brunswick*, p. 87; and Reynolds, "Babcock Tragedy," p. 218.
3. A description of Hanington's home can be found in Bell, *History of Old Shediac*.

The Messenger

1. Mary Hanington's signature appears on Jonathon Babcock's bail bond and release on his own recognizances, NBMA, S181 F107.2.
2. Photographs and a brief history of Younglands can be found in Maurice A. Leger and Ronnie-Gilles LeBlanc, *Historic Shediac* (Halifax, NS: Nimbus Publishing, 2003).
3. "unbarked logs" — Webster, *History of Shediac*, p. 3.
4. The location and description of the home of Mary and William Hanington are from Bell, *History of Old Shediac*.
5. The story of the midnight visit to Hanington's home is detailed in Reynolds, "Babcock Tragedy," p. 217.
6. "it was all a delusion, they wanted mad houses, not meeting houses," ibid.
7. "something to say before they die and they want it written down" — Lawrence, *Judges of New Brunswick*, p. 86. It is interesting to note that with the exception of a few direct quotes, the anecdote detailed in Lawrence is essentially a reprint of that in Reynolds, "Babcock Tragedy." Although Lawrence provides no specific references, those quotes appear to have come (in somewhat altered form) from his unpublished interview with William Hanington Jr. in the later years of his life, NBMA, S204-1 F6-3.
8. "perhaps I can convince them of their error" — Lawrence, *Judges of New Brunswick*, p. 86.

Hellfire

1. The signature of John Welling is from Jonathon Babcock's bail bond, NBMA, S181 F107.2.
2. Biographical details of John Welling II are from his genealogy, recorded by the United Empire Loyalists' Association of Canada.
3. For Welling's Shediac land grant, see PANB, F16303.
4. The details of the February 12, 1805, revival are from William Hanington's transcription of the event, NBMA, S181 F107.6. Additional details are from Hanington, letter to Botsford, February 21, 1805, NBMA, S181 F107.7. Quotes attributed to Samuel Cornwall are from his written statement, included in the text of the indictment of Jacob Peck, NBMA, S181 F109.2.
5. "saw the French all going down to hell" — Hanington, letter to Botsford, February 21, 1805, NBMA, S181 F107.7.
6. "cannot you pray for their immortal souls?," ibid.
7. "belongs to me and the Lord. She is an Angel of light" — from a witness

statement by Samuel Cornwall, cited in Peck's indictment for blasphemy and sedition, NBMA, S181 F109.2.

8. "I am bound here; there is my epistle. There is John the Baptist" — Hanington, letter to Botsford, February 21, 1805, NBMA, S181 F107.7.

9. "from them, I shall break and take my text" — from Peck's indictment, NMBA, S181 F109.2.

10. Although a highly detailed source, Hanington's letter to Botsford is problematic in that it collapses a number of revivals into one account, with little regard for maintaining an accurate timeline. As such, some details remain unclear. A number of revivals led up to the prophesies of February 12, and it is difficult at times to be certain to which revival he was referring. Furthermore, Hanington makes reference to a number of individuals as being present at one or more of the revivals. The congregants here listed as present are those known to have attended on February 12; the actual number of revivalists might have been higher. Finally, interpretation of the letter is confounded by Hanington's habit of referring to three different people as "Masa": Amos Babcock, his daughter Dorcas, and the victim, Mercy Hall. Careful parsing of the document, aided by comparison to the transcript of the revival, makes clear that it is Mercy who was described in the fateful prophesy, not Sarah Babcock, as postulated by Bell, *Newlight Baptist Journals*, p. 337.

11. "had seen her Sealed to Everlasting Destruction" — Hanington, letter to Botsford, February 21, 1805, NBMA, S181 F107.7.

12. "not to be in her senses" — Hanington's transcript of the prophesies, NBMA, S181 F107.6.

13. "Jacob Peck would say 'she will prophecy this or that'," ibid.

14. "this world would be drowned" — Hanington's transcript of the prophesies, NBMA, S181 F107.6.

15. "Did not come from God & that it hurt her Soul," ibid.

16. "it was not Lucy she meant?," ibid.

17. "Saviour would be born of a woman & laid in a manger in swaddling clothes," ibid.

18. "it is likely the end of the world will be this night. The Angel of the Lord is gone out to seal the people" — quoted in Peck's indictment, NBMA, S181 F109.2.

19. Slightly differing versions of the Mercy prophesy appear in both Hanington's letter to Botsford (February 21, 1805, NBMA, S181 F107.7) and the transcription of the February 12 revival (NBMA, S181 F107.6), but the points of incongruence are minor and do not affect the interpretation of the relevant passages.

20. Peck's prophesy about the end of crowned heads in Europe is described in Hanington, letter to Botsford, February 21, 1805, NBMA, S181 F107.7.

21. One reason to approach Reynolds's 1898 article with caution is revealed in

how Reynolds recounts the February 12 revival, an event to which he gives little heed, in which he references only the quote, "There is my epistle" ("Babcock Tragedy," p. 218). Reynolds argues that the only relevance of the revival to the Babcock tragedy was that the girls were trying to convert Hanington and the French; he makes no mention of the prophesies, the End of Days, or of statements relating to Mercy Hall.

22. Another warning flag is that Reynolds mistakenly identifies the Babcock daughter as Sarah. Babcock did have a daughter named Sarah, but she was only three years old in 1805. Bell (*Newlight Baptist Journals*) draws attention to Reynolds's error, incorrectly changing the name of the prophet to Mary. Babcock also had a daughter named Mary, but she was barely seven years of age at the time of the killing. The only teenaged Babcock daughter at the time was Dorcas, who was fifteen in 1805.

Grist for the Mill

1. Jonathon Babcock's signature is from his 1803 land grant petition, PANB, F1043.
2. Jonathon provided a detailed description of the night's events during the coroner's inquest, later presented to the grand jury; see NBMA, Government Collection, S181 F107.8.
3. "some great thing is going to happen tonight," ibid.
4. "the Lord should come to call the people to judgment," ibid.
5. "desired him to stop to pray for he was tired & sleepy," ibid.
6. "appeared to be much distressed in his mind & Groaned often," ibid.
7. "this is the bread of heaven" — This quote comes not from Jonathon's account but from Reynolds, "Babcock Tragedy," p. 218. Reynolds presumably relied on Dorcas Babcock's written statement, the only other eyewitness account recorded. There are a number of significant differences between Dorcas's and Jonathon's accounts, which is typical in cases of multiple witnesses describing the same event.
8. "Oh Lord, not only my head and hands but my feet also" — Jonathon's witness statement, NBMA, S181 F107.8.
9. "I see the stars falling from heaven," ibid. In Reynolds's account ("Babcock Tragedy," p. 218), Amos is quoted as saying, "The world is to end! The world is to end! The stars are falling."

End Times

1. "Be of good cheer" — Jonathon's witness statement, written during the coroner's inquest and later submitted to the grand jury, NBMA, S181 F107.8.
2. "to put their trust in God," ibid.
3. "I see them coming" and "it will be but a few minutes before they will be here," ibid.

Notes

4. "was a Cross," ibid.
5. Reynolds ("Babcock Tragedy," p. 219) claims that Amos called out "it is the cross of Christ" before stamping on the blade and whetstone.
6. "anointing" — Jonathon Babcock witness statement, NBMA, S181 F107.8.
7. "Gideon's men," ibid.
8. "make herself ready," ibid. Reynolds claims that Mercy was told to remove her dress ("Babcock Tragedy," p. 219), as do all subsequent reports. However, Jonathon's account clearly states she was told to remove only her shoes.
9. "would run her through" — Jonathon Babcock witness statement, NBMA, S181 F107.8.
10. "in the name of the Lord God of Israel," ibid.
11. According to his statement, Jonathon did not actually witness Amos stab Mercy. The description of the blows comes from the coroner's autopsy report, NBMA, OS F55.8. The coroner, Gideon Palmer, also took the now-lost witness statement of Dorcas Babcock and derived the sequence of blows from her eyewitness account.
12. "screeched out" — Jonathon Babcock witness statement, NBMA, S181 F107.8. Although he claimed to have left the cabin before the fatal blows were struck, he reported hearing Mercy's shriek as he ran for help.

Raising the Alarm
1. "saw the blood flow" — Reynolds, "Babcock Tragedy," p. 219.
2. "heard the Deceased Screech out" — Jonathon Babcock witness statement, NBMA, S181 F107.8.
3. "Alarmed the Neighbours," ibid.
4. "where he aroused the inmates" — Reynolds, "Babcock Tragedy," p. 219.
5. The map is an amalgamation of a number of sources, including a plot of Shediac showing all homesteads, in NBMA, William Lusk Webster Collection, S204-1 F10. Additional information regarding the specific location of houses circa 1805 is from Webster, *History of Shediac*, p. 15; Bell, *History of Old Shediac*; and the relevant deeds, mortgages, and leases for Westmorland County, 1767-1853, Harriet Irving Library, Loyalist Collection, FC LPR.N4L3W5D4.
6. "a Jacob Peck & Mansfield Cornwall" — William Hanington, letter to William Black, a justice for Westmorland County, February 14, 1805, NBMA, S181 F107.5.
7. Although Lawrence is the primary author of *The Judges of New Brunswick and Their Times*, the account of the Babcock tragedy in all likelihood was added by one of the posthumous editors of the work.
8. "Mr. Hanington told him he was as guilty as his brother." — Lawrence, *Judges of New Brunswick*, p. 87.
9. A partial transcript of the interview with William Hanington Jr. is

included in the notes on his father, NBMA, William Lusk Webster Collection, S204-1 F7.

10. "a sort of clerk of the peace" — John Edward Belliveau, *Running Far In: The Story of Shediac* (Halifax, NS: Nimbus Publishing, 2003), p. 36.

11. A chronological listing of all of William Hanington's parish officer appointments is in the Westmorland County General Record Book, Harriet Irving Library, LPR.N4P8W4L6. By the same token, it offers irrefutable proof that Hanington held no judicial or law enforcement office of any kind, as any such appointment would have been faithfully recorded in its pages.

12. Shediac's 1825 declaration as a parish is noted in Webster, *History of Shediac*, p. 15.

13. "the french people" — Hanington, letter to Black, February 14, 1805, NBMA, S181 F107.5.

The Arrest

1. "I found the prisoner standing" — Hanington, letter to Black, February 14, 1805, NBMA, S181 F107.5.

2. "On entering the house" — Reynolds, "Babcock Tragedy," p. 220.

3. "The prisoner, with his arms," ibid.

4. Jonathon Babcock witness statement, NBMA, S181 F107.8.

5. William Hanington identified Amasa Killam and Simeon Jenks as key to the search for Mercy's body; letter to Black, February 14, 1805, NBMA, S181 F107.5.

6. "I forgot to mention he had dragged the body of the deceased out of his house and buried it in the snow," ibid.

The Abyss

1. William Reynolds's signature is taken from an invoice he submitted in 1878, NBMA, CB DOC item 9.

2. In fact, "here, there be dragons" appears on only one historical map, the copper Lenox Globe, ca. 1500. The inscription, translated from its original Latin, is described in B.F. da Costa, "The Lenox Globe," *Magazine of American History* 3, no. 9 (1879): 529-540.

3. John W. Lawrence's tenure as president of the New Brunswick Historical Society is detailed in New Brunswick Historical Society Fonds, 1874-1969, NBMA, S25-29 F1-303.

4. "a speaker of more than ordinary ability" — obituary of J.W. Lawrence, *Saint John Daily Sun,* November 7, 1892.

5. A full text version of the inaugural issue of *New Brunswick Magazine,* featuring a reprint of "The Babcock Tragedy," is available online at http://archive.org/stream/newbrunswickmaga01stjouoft/newbrunswickmaga01stjouoft_djvu.txt.

6. "Through the aid of Rev. W.O. Raymond" — Reynolds, "Babcock Tragedy," p. 214.
7. It is important to note that William Hanington wrote a number of documents relating to this case. Three survive in the public record: 1) his first letter to Justice William Black; 2) a letter/witness statement regarding the actions of Jacob Peck; and 3) his transcript of Peck's revival and the prophesies of the Babcock child. The official witness statement of William Hanington, detailing his full involvement in the case, remains missing and is, in all likelihood, among the documents referenced in Reynolds, "Babcock Tragedy."
8. As for why these three statements were separated from the other witness accounts, they do have one thing in common: the statements of Killam, Hanington, and Dorcas Babcock were those used to indict Jacob Peck, as noted in the true bill (NBMA, S181 F109.2). It is possible these statements were separated by Ward Chipman or other court officials after Babcock's trial, in anticipation of their continued use in Peck's ongoing legal proceedings. After Peck's case limped to its inevitable conclusion, the three statements likely were never returned to the Babcock file, leaving them open to being "borrowed" by historians looking for information on the case.
9. "there remained much for Dr. Stockton to do" — Raymond, preface, in *Judges of New Brunswick*, p. i.
10. The story behind the writing of *The Judges of New Brunswick and Their Times* is detailed in the preface to the book, written by W.O. Raymond on September 26, 1907.
11. The collected papers of Raymond, Stockton, and Lawrence are part of LAC, Ward Chipman (Senior and Junior) Collection, R5176-0-0-E. Separate collections for Lawrence, Raymond, and Reynolds are also held at the NBMA.

Damages
1. The signature of Amasa Killam is from the court document releasing Jonathon Babcock on his own recognizances, NBMA, S181 F107.2
2. The reference to Hanington's letter relates to the missive addressed to Black, February 14, 1805, NBMA, S181 F107.5.
3. "strongly ironed in the dungeon" — Coroner Gideon Palmer, letter to Amos Botsford, February 20, 1805, NBMA, OS F55.8.
4. "Babcock was then taken to the house of Amasa Killam" — Reynolds, "Babcock Tragedy," p. 221
5. The Babcock transfer story in Lawrence, *Judges of New Brunswick*, pp. 88-89.
6. "on the way he broke loose but was recaptured" — Webster, *History of Shediac*, p. 15.

7. Webster's exhaustive research notes are housed in NBMA, William Lusk Webster Collection, S 204-1.
8. "once, when the sled overturned" — Belliveau, *Running Far In*, p. 36
9. "fit" and "the home of another of those who'd been 'revivalled'" — Grant, *Six for the Hangman*, p. 99.
10. "religious fit" — Allison Finnamore, *East Coast Murders: Mysteries, Crimes and Scandals* (Canmore, AB: Altitude Publishing, 2005), p. 60.
11. "the rest of the trip was uneventful," ibid.
12. For Amasa Killam's land grant petitions, see PANB, F1043 and F4171.

Dorchester
1. The signature by Robert Keillor is from one of his student notebooks, dated 1782, when Robert was eighteen years of age; Trueman Family Fonds, Mount Allison University Library Archives, Reference no. 0102, 1/9
2. Keillor's love of drink is expressed in a personal communication by W. Eugene Goodrich, past president of the Westmorland Historical Society and author of the Keillor House Museum's docent guide ("The Keillors of Keillor House")
3. Keillor's licence to operate a tavern is documented in the Records of the General Session of the Peace for Westmorland County, 1785-1809, Harriet Irving Library, LPR.N4P8W4L6.
4. Biographical details of the Keillor family are from Goodrich, "The Keillors of Keillor House."
5. For the Keillor brothers' 1786 petition for a land grant and that of lead petitioner Amos Botsford, see PANB, F1030; for the land grant award, see PANB, F16300.
6. The marriage of Robert and Ann is among the first recorded in the Marriage Registry of Westmorland County, Harriet Irving Library, N4C6S4W4M3R4.
7. John Keillor's ambitions and his land grant to secure the location of the Dorchester Courthouse are detailed in Goodrich, "The Keillors of Keillor House," pp. 2-7.
8. "in consideration of" — Keillor's December 22, 1802, deed, in ibid., p. 5.
9. Robert Keillor's service as constable for Dorchester is noted in the Records of the General Sessions of the Peace for Westmorland County, Harriet Irving Library, LPR.N4P8W4L6.
10. "strongly ironed in the dungeon" — Gideon Palmer, letter to Amos Botsford, February 20, 1805, NBMA, OS F55.1.
11. "accidental discovery" — Ward Chipman, draft of opening statement in the trial of Amos Babcock, LAC, R5176-0-0-E, 65.

Charnel House

1. Gideon Palmer's signature is from his letter to Botsford, February 20, 1805, NBMA, OS F55.1.

2. Biographical details of Gideon Palmer are from David A. Walker, "Ancestral Trails — Biography of Gideon Palmer" (electronic document, http://www.ancestraltrails.ca/walker%20for%20web-o/p732.htm#i268; accessed January 25, 2012), later confirmed through parish records. Additional information is from newspaper accounts and family obituaries, *Chignecto Post*, June 24, 1880, and July 18, 1889; and *Saint John Globe*, July 2, 1880.

3. "you're a liar" — from the obituary of John Palmer printed in the *Chignecto Post* on July 18, 1889.

4. For Palmer's land grant, see PANB, F16300.

5. Details of Palmer's inquest are contained in his report, NBMA, OS F55.8.

6. Although Dorcas Babcock's witness statement is now lost, its existence is noted in Palmer's inquest report. Jonathon's witness statement, also taken during Palmer's inquest, survives in NBMA, S181 F107.8.

7. The inventory of Amos Babcock's estate can be found in the records of the Executive Council, 1787-1851, Harriet Irving Library, FC LPR.N4E9T7.

8. "The Frenchmen" — Gideon Palmer uses the term "frenchman" in his letter to Botsford, February 20, 1805, NBMA, OS F55.1. He was not alone in the practice; Hanington refers to the Acadians as "french people" in his letter to Black, February 14, 1805, NBMA, S181 F107.5.

9. The list of coroner's jury members is from the coroner's report, NBMA, OS F55.8.

10. "a gentleman, one of the coroners of our Lord" and "Masala Hall there and then lying dead," ibid.

11. "I have the knife" — Hanington, postscript to letter to Black, February 14, 1805, NBMA, S181 F107.5.

12. "a certain knife of the value of six pence" — Palmer, report, NBMA, OS F55.8.

13. The description of Mercy's wounds comes from ibid.

14. "If you proffer" — Palmer, letter to Botsford, February 20, 1805, NBMA, S181 F107.1.

15. Davison's 1808 murder is noted in documents in NBMA, Hugh T. Hazen Collection, S65 F90.11.

16. Palmer's invoices and compensation for his services in the Babcock investigation were duly noted in the Westmorland Local Records, 1751-1883, Harriet Irving Library, Loyalist Collection, LPR.N4P8W4L6.

The Long Ride Home

1. There were no formal burial grounds or churches in Shediac Parish in 1805. Tradition held that burials take place on family land. As neither

Amos nor Jonathon had successfully drawn land in the granting system, the family owned no property. Oral history suggests Jonathon simply buried her on the property he occupied and farmed. The period also predates the practice of publishing an obituary in the newspaper.

The Accusation

1. For Hanington's transcript, see NBMA, S181 F107.6.
2. For Gideon Palmer's final inquest report, see NBMA, OS F55.
3. "his dust reposes at the Dorchester Cemetery" — brief biographical sketch of Palmer, published as part of his son's obituary, *Chignecto Post*, June 24, 1880.
4. "I have related the heads of things" — Hanington, letter to Botsford, February 21, 1805, NBMA, S181 F107.7.
5. "PS — the gentlemen of the Jury are now waiting for this letter," ibid.
6. Which people filled Hanington's house is unclear. If any of the coroner's jury members accompanied Hanington and Palmer back to his home at Shediac Cape, Hanington does not mention them by name in his account.

A Lesser Evil

1. The signature of Amos Botsford is from a letter to J.W. Lawrence, NBMA, Hugh T. Hazen Collection, S65 F100.15.
2. The signature of William Botsford appears on a letter to John Keillor, March 5, 1811, NBMA, Government Collection, S13 F180.2.
3. "The Hanington letter" — quoted in Bell, *Newlight Baptist Journals*, p. 332.
4. Biographical details of Amos and William Botsford are from the Botsford Family History, Botsford Family Collection, NBMA, S123-1. Additional information is from obituaries and estate notices published in *Chignecto Post*, March 22, 1894; *Daily Telegraph*, May 21, 1864; *Gleaner*, June 25, 1891; *Loyalist*, August 7, 1845; *New Brunswick Royal Gazette*, September 21, 1812, and March 22, 1813; *New Brunswick Courier*, May 14, 1864; and *New Brunswick Reporter and Fredericton Advisor*, November 28, 1882.
5. The strange tale of the first murder in New Brunswick history, the killing of John Mosely, is recounted at length in "A Fork to the Head."
6. David Nelson's and William Harboard's appointments as Queen's Rangers are in the Muster Roll of Loyalist Troops, 1780, NBMA, S26 F6 VI.
7. The specifics of the case against Nelson and Harboard are from Lawrence, *Judges of New Brunswick*, pp. 61-63, which reprints key court documents — including David Nelson's witness statement of May 24, 1786 — in their entirety.
8. The ire and reaction of the First Nations community is described in Edward Winslow, letter to Ward Chipman, May 25, 1786, reprinted in ibid., pp. 62-63.

9. "two men of fair character should be sacrificed to satisfy the barbarous claims of a set of savages," ibid.

True Bills

1. Christopher Horsman's appearance on the grand jury and the identity of the other jury members are documented in NBMA, S181 F107.4. As a matter of expediency, the same jury heard the evidence against both Babcock and Peck.

2. That grand jury testimony used written statements, rather than direct eyewitness testimony, is confirmed in the postscript of a letter written by William Hanington, NBMA, S181 F107.7.

3. The identities and order of appearance of the witnesses are recorded in the respective indictments of Babcock (NBMA, S181 F07.3) and Peck (NBMA, S181 F109.2).

4. "Bloody Code" — a widely adopted euphemism for English criminal law — made a staggeringly high number of relatively minor offences punishable by death. The history of the code and its colourful euphemism are related in J.H. Baker, *An Introduction to English Legal History*, 4th ed. (New York: Oxford University Press, 2005); John Briggs, *Crime and Punishment in England: An Introductory History* (New York: St. Martin's Press, 1996); and Deanna Foster, *A History of Hangings in Nova Scotia* (Lawrencetown, NS: Pottersfield Press, 2007).

5. "to take, embezzle and steal a quantity of twist" — *The Crown v. Higgins* (1801), 2 East 5, 102 E.R. 269, cited in *The Commonwealth v. Randolph* (Pennsylvania), 1892.

Guaranteed

1. The signature of Leonard Peck is from an 1810 land grant petition, PANB, F4174.

2. "commanding the Constables of Dorchester" — arrest warrant of Jacob Peck, NBMA, Government Collection, S181 F109.1.

3. The names of the Dorchester constables are from a list of Constables by Parish, Babcock murder file, NBMA, S181 F107.4 (a) and (d).

4. "blasphemous and seditious language" — indictment of Jacob Peck, NBMA, S181 F109.2.

5. "Jacob Peck, late of the Parish of Dorchester," ibid.

6. "derision and contempt for the Christian religion," ibid.

7. The amount of the bond and the identities of the sureties are from the writ releasing Jacob Peck on his own recognizances issued by Justice Watson, NBMA, S181 F109.3.

8. Biographic details of Reuben Mills are from the probate records of his estate, described in R. Wallace Hale, *Early New Brunswick Probate Records, 1785-1835* (Bowie, MD: Heritage Books, 1989); and from the

General Record Book of Westmorland County, 1751-1883, Harriet Irving Library, Loyalist Collection, LPR.N4P8W4L6.

9. "-1- that Jacob Peck shall personally appear" — the conditions of Peck's release are from Watson's writ of release, NBMA, S181 F109.3.

Material Witness

1. This muddled signature by Jonathon Babcock is affixed to his bail bond, NBMA, S181 F107.2. It offers a fascinating glimpse into Jonathon's anxious and chaotic state of mind at the time he signed his release.
2. For the indictment of Amos Babcock, see NBMA, S181 F107.3.
3. "lawful money" —Jonathon Babcock bail notice, NBMA, S181 F107.2.
4. "the nature of this obligation," ibid.
5. Hezekiah King consistently refers to Amos and Mercy by their proper given names throughout the minutes of the trial; see Proceedings of the Courts of Nisi Prius, Oyer and Terminer and Gaol Delivery of the Province of New Brunswick for the year 1786 to 1808, PANB, RS36 A1.
6. The condition of the bond and the names and signatures of the sureties are found on the writ — ibid.
7. For lively discussions of common law and the practices regarding spousal testimony, see Baker, *Introduction to English Legal History*; *Blackstone's Commentaries on the Laws of England* (New Haven, CT: Yale Law School, Lillian Goldman Law Library, 1765); Allyson May, *The Bar and the Old Bailey: 1750-1850* (Chapel Hill: University of North Carolina Press, 2003); and John McLaren, *Dewigged, Bothered and Bewildered: British Colonial Judges on Trial, 1800-1900* (Toronto: University of Toronto Press, 2011).

Jurisprudent

1. Judge Upham's signature appears on a letter to Chief Justice George Duncan Ludlow, NBMA, F96.6.
2. The descriptions of Upham's troubles with rheumatoid arthritis, the poor roads, and the travel conditions along the circuit are from a letter to Ward Chipman, October 17, 1792, reprinted in Lawrence, *Judges of New Brunswick*, p. 82.
3. The salaries of Supreme Court justices in 1805 were a matter of public record, published in the very documents that granted them their authority, as well as discussed in Upham, letter to Ward Chipman, 1808, NBMA, S38-1 F20.7.
4. Biographical details of Joshua Upham are from letters by him to Henry Knox, December 1, 1783 (Massachusetts Historical Society); Timothy Pickering, November 18, 1783 (LAC); and Edward Winslow, 1783 (University of New Brunswick Library), as well as from a letter about Upham written by Thomas Carleton in 1793 (NBMA). Additional details were drawn from the chapter on Upham in Lawrence, *Judges of New Brunswick*.

Notes

5. Details of Upham's land grants are from the 1785 and 1786 grants, PANB, F16302, F16300.
6. Upham related the bridge mishap in open court during Babcock's trial; court minutes, PANB, RS36 A1.
7. The Supreme Court slavery decision is discussed at length in Lawrence, *Judges of New Brunswick*, pp. 74-75. For the majority opinion, written by Chief Justice George Duncan Ludlow, see NBMA, S64 F59.23.
8. "if he thought Master would sell him, he would kill him" — quoted in Lawrence, *Judges of New Brunswick*, p. 92.
9. Details of the murder of Alice West and the trial of Luke Hamilton are from the testimony of Luke Hamilton, NBMA, S65 F92.16(2); the indictment of Hamilton in 1799, NBMA, S65 F92.16(1); and the coroner's inquest of Alice West, NBMA, S65 F90.7.
10. "no slave owners admitted" — cited in Dan Soucoup, *Historic New Brunswick* (Lawrencetown, NS: Pottersfield Press, 1997), which also includes a thoughtful discussion on the end of slavery in New Brunswick.

A Fork to the Head

1. "Aha! Aha! Aha! It was permitted!" — quoted in Reynolds, "Babcock Tragedy," p. 221.
2. "might have thought under his delusion" — Ward Chipman, pre-trial notes, LAC, R5176-0-0-E, 65; emphasis added.
3. The history and specifics of the benefits of clergy are recounted in Richard B. Morris, "The Benefits of Clergy in America and Related Matters," *University of Pennsylvania Law Review* 105 (1957): 436. A discussion of the provision specific to New Brunswick courts is found in Lawrence, *Judges of New Brunswick*, pp. 27-29.
4. "Agreeable to your request" —Samuel Moore's inquest of John Mosely, reprinted in Lawrence, *Judges of New Brunswick*, p. 25.
5. "that the fork was the occasion of his death" — Amos Sheffield's jury verdict, reprinted in ibid.
6. The outcome of the Mosely case is recorded on the List of Prisoners Confined in the Gaol at Parr Town, January 17, 1785, NBMA, S65 F96.1.
7. The Ordinance for establishing the Supreme Court of New Brunswick is in the Hugh T. Hazen Collection, NBMA, S64 F59.22.

Of Traitors and Tribulations

1. Ward Chipman's signature appends a letter to the mayor of Saint John, November 18, 1823, NBMA, S36 F11.11.
2. Biographical details of Ward Chipman Sr. and Jr. are from the Ward Chipman (Senior and Junior) Fonds, LAC, R5176-0-0-E.
3. Details of *Benedict Arnold v. Monson Hayt* are drawn from the Benedict Arnold and Monson Hayt Fonds, University of New Brunswick Library

Archives, MG HS F1-7, and the Benedict Arnold Papers, 1741-1801, NBMA, S29 C.

Indefensible

1. "if you cannot afford an attorney" — This crime show staple is derived from the landmark case *Miranda v. Arizona*, 384 U.S. 436 (1966), which mandates that an arresting officer read the detainee his or her rights. The Canadian Criminal Code contains no such provision. Peace officers in Canada are required only to offer detainees the phone number of a legal aid lawyer on duty, who can give limited counsel and who provides referrals to lawyers in the accused's area.

2. Further to the rights to defence counsel in Canada, section 10 of the Canadian Charter of Rights and Freedoms, enacted in 1982, stipulates that a person placed under arrest has the right to retain and instruct counsel at his or her own expense, although a suspect does not have the right to have counsel present during questioning. No such stipulation existed in 1805. Anyone had the right to question Babcock or Peck at any time and in any manner he or she chose.

3. Chipman's pre-trial notes are in LAC, Ward Chipman (Senior and Junior) Fonds, R5176-0-0-E; they are also reproduced in a slightly redacted form in Bell, *Newlight Baptist Journals*, pp. 342-344.

4. "drunkenness is no excuse," ibid.

5. "tho' it may make a man so mad," ibid.

6. "a mental disorder that rendered the person incapable" — from John A. Yogis, ed., *Barron's Canadian Law Dictionary*, 5th ed. (Hauppauge, NY: Barron's Educational, 2003), p. 174. The entry also includes a discussion of the history of the definition of insanity in Canadian courts and the specifics of the common law test for mental disorders.

7. "If insanity is his defense" — Chipman, pre-trial notes, LAC, R5176-0-0-E.

8. "Madness...whether permanent or temporary must be unequivocal & plain," ibid.; emphasis in original.

9. "in all very atrocious crimes," ibid.

10. "any idle wild fanatic opinion," ibid.

11. "It is astonishing that the mild religion of the Gospel," ibid.

12. "If ignorant and weak minds by indulging in reveries of this kind," ibid., emphasis added.

13. "with regard to those whose coming is after the working of Satan," ibid.; emphasis in original.

Merits and Demerits

1. All pre-trial motions and the events of June 13 and 14 are faithfully recorded in the Minutes of the Proceedings of the Courts of Nisi Prius,

Oyer and Terminer and Gaol Delivery of the Province of New Brunswick for the years 1786 to 1808, PANB, RS36 A1.

2. "in a very pointed manner," ibid., p. 287.

Plea in Suspension

1. The trials of Jacob Peck and Amos Babcock are detailed in the Minutes of the Proceedings of the Courts of Nisi Prius, PANB, RS36 A1.
2. "on account of the absence of material witnesses," ibid., p. 289.
3. Bell (*Newlight Baptist Journals*, p. 334) identifies Peck's second surety as John McDonald; yet, according to the Minutes of the Proceedings, the man's name was Daniel.

The Burden of Proof

1. The timetable of the day's events is documented in the Minutes of the Proceedings of the Courts of Nisi Prius, Oyer and Terminer and Gaol Delivery of the Province of New Brunswick, 1786 to 1808, PANB, RS36 A1.
2. "I shall make no comments upon the facts" — Chipman, pre-trial notes, LAC, R5176-0-0-E, 65.
3. "the supposed former grudge" and "with caution," ibid.; original emphasis.
4. "that the deceased was considered a reprobate," ibid.
5. "was permitted" — quote attributed to Amos Babcock, cited in Reynolds, "Babcock Tragedy," p. 221.
6. "accidental discovery" — Chipman, pre-trial notes, LAC, R5176-0-0-E, 65.
7. That Babcock's defence focused on the prophesies is evident in the media account of the case, published in the *Royal Gazette,* June 26, 1805.
8. Babcock's defence witnesses are listed in the minutes of the court. Among the tasks of the clerk of the court, Hezekiah King, was to record the timeline of the trial. As such, there were specific notes as to when court was called to session and adjourned and how long the jury deliberated.
9. "leave the cause with confidence" — Chipman, pre-trial notes, LAC, R5176-0-0-E, 65.
10. "The sentence of the court is" — noted in the Minutes of the Proceedings of the Courts of Nisi Prius, Oyer and Terminer and Gaol Delivery of the Province of New Brunswick, 1786 to 1808, PANB, RS36 A1.

Mortal Coils

1. John Jerome made his mark at the end of his statement/confession, penned by Justice Samuel Gay following his arrest in February 1805, NBMA, S181 F108.1.
2. Laws and practices relating to the execution of prisoners by hanging are detailed in Briggs, *Crime and Punishment in England*; and Foster, *History of Hangings in Nova Scotia.*
3. Jerome's shackled incarceration, as well as his age and the fact that he

"stole a horse from a Frenchman," are noted in Palmer, letter to Botsford, February 20, 1805, NBMA, S181 F107.1.

4. The details of Jerome's crimes are taken from his indictment (S181 F108.1); the true bill issued by the grand jury (S181 F108.2); the warrant issued to search William Wellington's home (S181 F108.3); and Jerome's statement (S181 F108.5), NBMA.

5. "was in his liquor" — Jerome, witness statement, NBMA, S181 F108.5.

6. "during the short but awful interval" — *Blackstone's Commentaries.*

A Discernible Shift

1. "The hanging took place as scheduled" — Webster, *History of Shediac*, p. 16.

2. "It appeared in evidence that for some time" — *Royal Gazette*, June 26, 1805; emphasis in original.

3. Bell (*Newlight Baptist Journals*, p. 345) concurs that Chipman was the likely author of the *Royal Gazette* article, although he sees the thrust of the article as "the cautionary effect it might have on a public increasingly tempted to forsake the Church of England for religious dissent."

4. "The above named Jacob Peck" — *Royal Gazette*, June 26, 1805; emphasis in original.

5. The probate records of Dorcas's father, Caleb Bennett, are reprinted in Hale, *Early New Brunswick Probate Records*, p. 336.

6. Caleb and Henry Babcock appear in the 1820 census of Sackville. Henry is listed as single, Caleb as a widower with one child.

7. According to his tombstone, Caleb Babcock died on February 18, 1878, at age eighty-five; he is buried at the Four Corners' Cemetery, Upper Sackville, NB.

8. Elizabeth Babcock Sears died in Saint John in 1849 but is buried with her husband at the Riverview Cemetery, Edgett's Landing, Albert County, NB. Benjamin Bennett, Dorcas Babcock's brother, is also buried there. He died on March 16, 1858, at the age of ninety-four.

9. The location of Jonathon Babcock's grave is unknown. His son, Jonathon Jr., died on January 23, 1857, and is buried in Wilson's Beach Cemetery, Campobello Island, NB.

10. The story of Hanington's later years is from Bell, *History of Old Shediac*. Additional details are from the Hanington Family Fonds, NBMA, 0.5 CB DOC.1; and the biography of Hanington, PANB, MC1286, vol. VII.

Hindsight

1. This, the final purported signature of Jacob Peck, is from his 1810 land grant petition, PANB, F4174 (Robert Scott, lead petitioner). The document was not signed publicly and Jacob's signature bears a striking similarity to

that of his brother, Leonard, which appears later in the same document and can be seen on page 139.

2. "There is nothing available" — Reynolds, "Babcock Tragedy," p. 222.

3. Grant's quotation is from *Six for the Hangman*, p. 100.

4. Finnamore's quotation is from *East Coast Murders*, p. 61.

5. Peck's marriage to Horsman is recorded in the marriage registry of Westmorland County, 1790-1835, Harriet Irving Library, Loyalist Collection, FC LPR.N4C6S4W4M3R4.

6. Peck's appointments to his various parish posts are documented in the Public Records of Westmorland County, 1751-1883, Harriet Irving Library, Loyalist Collection, C3201.

7. The gap in the historic record is evident in the surviving volumes of the Minutes and Records of the Supreme Court, Westmorland, PANB, RS42. Both books cover the period from 1785 to 1809; the next set of court records covers 1818 to 1824.

8. The forfeit of Peck's bail in 1809 was noted in the clerk's records of costs due to the court; NBMA, F100.9.

9. "thought it best to let the whole Babcock affair rest" — Bell, *Newlight Baptist Journals*, p. 334.

10. Details of Joshua Upham's journey and his efforts to secure better pay are from his letter to Ward Chipman, 1808, PANB, S38-1 F20.7. The incident is also recounted in Lawrence, *Judges of New Brunswick*, p. 89.

11. "a large family of children, many of them very young, without any means of support" — quoted in Lawrence, *Judges of New Brunswick*, p. 90.

12. Ward Chipman's appointment to the Supreme Court is documented in his commission, NBMA, OS F21.1.

13. For Peck's 1810 petition for land, see PANB, F4174 (Robert Scott, lead petitioner).

14. "which would prevent many disturbing stances," ibid.

15. The Crown's response to the petition, dated August 11, 1820, is in ibid.

16. For the note discussing *Christian Steeves v. Jacob Peck*, see PANB, RS42 1823.

17. Evidence of Steeves's place of residence is drawn from a deed dated 1807, NBMA, S180 F57.16; and from articles in the *Chignecto Times* (1884), *Saint John Daily Telegraph* (1884), and *Christian Visitor* (1878).

18. The history of Burnt Hills and record of Leonard Peck's interment are from notes in the Westmorland Cemetery Records, James Humphreys Collection, PANB, MC600 MS4 A and C.

19. Alternatively, Jacob Peck might be buried in the Blakney Pioneer Cemetery. Peck was a tenant on David Blakney's property in 1810 (as noted in Peck's last land grant petition, PANB, F4174) and the Blakney cemetery was the earliest burial ground for the English-speaking settlers in Salisbury Parish.

Postscript: *Quaeitur*

1. The history of Garrow's "innocent until proven guilty" axiom and its impact on the practise of law is chronicled at length in John Hostettler and Richard Braby, *Sir William Garrow: His Life, His Times and Fight for Justice* (Hampshire: Waterside Press, 2010); see also Kenneth Pennington, "Innocent until Proven Guilty: The Origins of a Legal Maxim," *Jurist* 63, no. 1 (2003): 106-124.

2. Counselling in acts of genocide is discussed in *Mugesera v. Canada* [2005] 2 S.C.R. 100, 2005 SCC44.

3. Hate crimes and propaganda are defined in the Criminal Code of Canada in section 319(1).

4. "Canadian criminal code has always" — Marilyn Pilon, "Mental Disorder and Canadian Criminal Law" (Ottawa: Library of Parliament, Parliamentary Research Branch, October 5, 1999; rev. January 22, 2002), p. 1.

5. "That a crazy man" — Reynolds, "Babcock Tragedy," p. 222.

6. "Contrasting this case" — Lawrence, *Judges of New Brunswick*, p. 89, although it was possibly written by Stockton or Raymond after Lawrence's death.

Bibliography

Babcock, Amos. Petition for a land grant in Westmorland County, 1803. Provincial Archives of New Brunswick, RS108 Index of Land Petitions, 1783-1918, F1043.

Babcock, Jonathon. 1805. Statement before the coroner's jury, 1805. Governmental Collection, New Brunswick Museum Archives, S181 F107.8.

Baker, J.H. *An Introduction to English Legal History*, 4th ed. New York: Oxford University Press, 2005.

Bell, David Graham. *Early Loyalist Saint John: The Origins of New Brunswick Politics, 1783-1786.* Fredericton, NB: New Ireland Press, 1983.

___. *Henry Alline and Maritime Religion.* Ottawa: Canadian Historical Association, 1993.

___. *Legal Education in New Brunswick: A History.* Fredericton: University of New Brunswick Press, 1992.

___. *Newlight Baptist Journals of James Manning and James Innis.* Saint John, NB: Acadia Divinity College and the Baptist Historical Committee, 1984.

Bell, Fannie Chandler. *A History of Old Shediac New Brunswick.* Moncton, NB: National Print, 1937.

Belliveau, John Edward. *Running Far In: The Story of Shediac.* Halifax, NS: Nimbus Publishing, 2003.

Black, Cyrus. *Historical Record of the Posterity of William Black.* Amherst, NS: Amherst Gazette Steam Printing House, 1885.

Black, William. Arrest warrant for Jacob Peck, February 22, 1805. Governmental Collection, New Brunswick Museum Archives, S181 F109.1.

___. Indictment, *King v. Jacob Peck*, February 23, 1805. Governmental Collection, New Brunswick Museum Archives, S181 F109.2.

Blackstone's Commentaries on the Laws of England. 1765. Available online at

Yale Law School, Lillian Goldman Law Library, http://avalon.law.yale.
edu/18th_century/blackstone_bk4ch14.asp; accessed February 4, 2012.

Botsford, Amos. Letter to J.W. Lawrence, December 2, 1778. Hugh T. Hazen
Collection, New Brunswick Museum Archives, S65 F100.15.

___. Petition for a land grant in Westmorland County (with Robert Keillor),
1786. Provincial Archives of New Brunswick, RS108 Index of Land
Petitions, 1783-1918, F1030.

Botsford, William. Letter to John Keillor, March 5, 1811. Governmental
Collection, New Brunswick Museum Archives, S13 F180.2.

Bottomley, John. 1992. "Songs with the Ornamental Hermits." Audio
recording. BMG Music Canada.

Boyle, Charles. Petition for a land grant in Westmorland County (with
Jonathon Babcock), 1798. Provincial Archives of New Brunswick, RS108
Index of Land Petitions, 1783-1918, F1040.

Briggs, John. *Crime and Punishment in England: An Introductory History*.
New York: St. Martin's Press, 1996.

Brooks, Anne. "Ancestry (Ann Horsman)," January 23, 2008. Available online
at http://www.annebrooks.ca/getperson.php?personID=I8089&tree=6126;
accessed March 9, 2012.

Broughton, Karen. *Cemeteries of Westmorland County, New Brunswick*.
Riverview, NB: New Brunswick Genealogical Society, Southeastern
Branch, 2008.

Bumsted, J.M. "Henry Alline." In *Dictionary of Canadian Biography*. Available
online at http://biographi.ca/009004-119.01-e.php?id_nbr=1731; accessed
November 13, 2011.

Camp, W. "An Historical Sketch of the First Hillsborough Baptist Church,"
1938. First Hillsborough Baptist Church Fonds, 1822-1926, New
Brunswick Museum Archives, CB DOC (two files).

Campbell, William. Testimony (examination) of Luke Hamilton, 1799. New
Brunswick Museum Archives, S65 F92.16(2).

Carleton, Thomas. Certificate attesting Joshua Upham as Justice of the
Supreme Court of New Brunswick, March 5, 1793. Jarvis Family Papers,
New Brunswick Museum Archives, S88-1 B27 F5 F179.5.

Chevalier, Heather. "Babcock Family Archives." January 6, 2001. Available
online: http://archiver.rootsweb.ancestry.com/th/read/
BABCOCK/2001-01/0978759046; accessed February 24, 2012.

___. "Babcock Genealogy." October 25, 2009. Available online: http://www.
genealogy.com/genealogy/users/c/h/e/Heather-Chevalier/; accessed
February 13, 2012.

Chignecto Post. "Biography of William Botsford," March 22, 1894. Provincial
Archives of New Brunswick, Daniel F. John's New Brunswick Newspaper
Vital Statistics Database, vol. 92, no. 2114, rank 60.

___. "Death notice of Trueman Steeves," November 6, 1884. Provincial

Archives of New Brunswick, Daniel F. John's New Brunswick Newspaper
Vital Statistics Database, vol. 62, no. 1707, rank 101.

____. "Gideon Palmer obituary," July 18, 1889. Provincial Archives of New
Brunswick, Daniel F. John's New Brunswick Newspaper Vital Statistics
Database, vol. 73, no. 341, rank 253.

____. Settlement of the estate of Gideon Palmer, June 24, 1880. Provincial
Archives of New Brunswick, Daniel F. John's New Brunswick Newspaper
Vital Statistics Database, vol. 54, no. 472, rank 152.

Chipman, Ward. Chipman's Process Book, 1785-1809, 1809. New Brunswick
Museum Archives, A73 S14.

____. Draft of opening remarks in the trial of Amos Babcock, 1805. Library and
Archives Canada, R5176-0-0-E, 65.

____. Letter to the Mayor of Saint John, November 18, 1823. Hugh T. Hazen
Collection, New Brunswick Museum Archives, S36 F11.11.

Christian Visitor. "Obituary of Christian Steeves," July 24, 1878. Provincial
Archives of New Brunswick, Daniel F. John's New Brunswick Newspaper
Vital Statistics Database, vol. 43, no. 2549, rank 76.

Coke, Edward. *The Institutes of the Laws of England*, part I. New York: Legal
Classics Library, 1823.

Consentino, Lucie LeBlanc. "Acadian and French Canadian Ancestral
Home — Shediac, New Brunswick." Available online: http://www.acadian-
home.org/shediac.html; accessed February 6, 2012.

da Costa, B.F. "The Lenox Globe." *Magazine of American History* 3, no. 9
(1879): 529-540.

Daily Telegraph. "Obituary of William Botsford," May 21, 1864. Provincial
Archives of New Brunswick, Daniel F. John's New Brunswick Newspaper
Vital Statistics Database, vol. 22, no. 1042, rank 60.

Dawson, Joan. *The Mapmaker's Legacy: Nineteenth-century Nova Scotia
through Maps*. Halifax: Nimbus Publishing, 2007.

Extracts of an interview with Judge Joshua Upham. Alice L. Fairweather Fonds,
New Brunswick Museum Archives, S191-1 F40.9.

Finnamore, Allison. *East Coast Murders: Mysteries, Crimes and Scandals*.
Canmore, AB: Altitude Publishing, 2005.

First Families. "Keillor Family." Provincial Archives of New Brunswick.
Available online: http://www.nbgs.ca/firstfamilies/FAMILY-K-2006.pdf;
accessed March 1, 2012.

Foster, Deanna. *A History of Hangings in Nova Scotia*. Lawrencetown, NS:
Pottersfield Press, 2007.

Garner, Bryan A. *Black's Law Dictionary*, 2nd ed. St. Paul, MN: West Group,
1996.

Gay, Samuel. Bench warrant for the arrest of John Jerome, 1805. Governmental
Collection, New Brunswick Museum Archives, S181 F108.3.

____. Examination of John Jerome on charges of theft, 1805. Governmental Collection, New Brunswick Museum Archives, S181 F108.2.

____. Indictment of John Jerome for burglary, February 9, 1805. Governmental Collection, New Brunswick Museum Archives, S181 F108.1.

____. Jerome held over for trial, 1805. New Brunswick Museum Archives, Governmental Collection, S181 F108.4.

"Gideon Palmer Genealogy." Available online: http://www.mulvihill.net/genealogy/fullfamil/pafg03.htm; accessed January 25, 2012.

Gleaner. "Obituary of Dr. George Botsford," June 25, 1891. Provincial Archives of New Brunswick, Daniel F. John's New Brunswick Newspaper Vital Statistics Database, vol. 78, no. 2615, rank 101.

Goodrich, W. Eugene. "The Keillors of Keillor House: A Guide for Guides." Dorchester, NB: Keillor House Museum, May, 2011.

Gordon, Greg. "Henry Alline — the Apostle of Nova Scotia." *Revival Preachers Circular* 5. Available online: http://www.calltoprayer.org.uk/revivalpreacher5.html; accessed November 13, 2011.

Grant, B.J. *Six for the Hangman*. Fredericton, NB: Fiddlehead Poetry Books and Goose Lane Editions, 1983.

Gray, Joseph. Petition for the regranting of the Hillsborough Grants, made to Joseph Gerrish, August 26, 1786. Manuscript collection, Fort Beauséjour-Fort Cumberland National Historic Site.

____. Return of inhabitants in the township of Hillsborough, June 1, 1783. William Frances Ganong Fonds, New Brunswick Musem Archives, OS F65.1.

Gross, Richard. Petition for a land grant in Albert County, 1809. Provincial Archives of New Brunswick, RS108 Index of Land Grants, 1783-1918, F4172.

Hale, R. Wallace. *Early New Brunswick Probate Records, 1785-1835*. Bowie, MD: Heritage Books, 1989.

Hanington, William. Letter to William Black, Esq., February 14, 1805. Governmental Collection, New Brunswick Museum Archives, S181 F107.5.

____. Letter to Amos Botsford, February 21, 1805. Governmental Collection, New Brunswick Museum Archives, S181 F107.7.

____. Transcript of Peck's revival, sent to the Justices of Westmorland County, February 1805. Governmental Collection, New Brunswick Museum Archives, S181 F107.6.

Harvard Law School. "Our History." Available online: http://www.law.harvard.edu/about/history.html; accessed January 28, 2012.

Hostettler, John, and Richard Braby. *Sir William Garrow: His Life, His Times and Fight for Justice*. Hampshire: Waterside Press, 2010.

Kanner, Ken. "Marriage Registries of Westmorland County, 1790-1856." Toronto: Metro Toronto Reference Library, 1986.

Keillor, Robert. Page from a student notebook, 1782. Trueman Family Fonds

1750-1931, Mount Allison University Library Archive, reference number 0102/1/9.

___. Petition for a land grant in Westmorland County, 1814. Provincial Archives of New Brunswick, RS108 Index of Land Petitions, 1783-1918, F4176.

Keillor House Museum. "Archival Holdings at Keillor House." Available online: http://www.keillorhousemuseum.com/geneology.htm

Kimball, Paul. "Amos Babcock...Crazed Murderer or...?" April 8, 2006. Available online: http://redstarfilms.blogspot.ca/2006/04/amos-babcock-crazed-murderer-or.html; accessed March 27, 2012.

King, Hezekiah. Release of Jonathon Babcock on his own recognizances, March 6, 1805. Governmental Collection, New Brunswick Museum Archives, S181 F107.2.

Law, James. Sworn statement regarding theft of property (John Jerome), 1805. Governmental Collection, New Brunswick Museum Archives, S181 F108.1.

Lawrence, Joseph W. *The Judges of New Brunswick and Their Times*, edited by A.A. Stockton and W.O. Raymond. Saint John, NB: Miramichi Books, 1915.

LeBlanc, Tony A. "The 1871 Census of Shediac Parish, Westmorland County, and Dunden Parish, Kent County of New Brunswick." Riverview, NB: Tony LeBlanc, 1996.

Leger, Maurice A., and Ronnie-Gilles LeBlanc. *Historic Shediac*. Halifax, NS: Nimbus Publishing, 2003.

Loyalist. "Prominent monuments of the Saint John burying ground," August 7, 1845. Provincial Archives of New Brunswick, Daniel F. John's New Brunswick Newspaper Vital Statistics Database, vol. 11, no. 334, rank 38.

Ludlow, George Duncan. Chief justice's opinion and arguments from slavery trial in New Brunswick, 1803. Hugh T. Hazen Collection, New Brunswick Museum Archives, S64 F 59.23.

Map of Shediac Parish with land allotments from 1800. William Lusk Webster Collection, New Brunswick Museum Archives, S204-1 F10.

May, Allyson. *The Bar and the Old Bailey: 1750-1850*. Chapel Hill: University of North Carolina Press, 2003.

McDonough, James T., ed. *Stedman's Concise Medical Dictionary*, 2nd ed. Baltimore: Williams and Wilkins, 1994.

McLaren, John. *Dewigged, Bothered and Bewildered: British Colonial Judges on Trial, 1800-1900*. Toronto: University of Toronto Press, 2011.

Mills, David. Petition for a land grant in Westmorland County, 1811. Provincial Archives of New Brunswick, RS108 Index of Land Petitions, 1783-1918, F4174.

Moncton Times. "Excerpts of 'The History of Henrick Steeves'," March 3, 1893. Provincial Archives of New Brunswick, Daniel F. John's New Brunswick Newspaper Vital Statistics Database, vol. 87, no. 5, rank 38.

Moore, Christopher. *The Law Society of Upper Canada and Ontario's Lawyers, 1797-1997*. Toronto: University of Toronto Press, 1997.

Morris, Richard B. "The Benefits of Clergy in America and Related Matters." *University of Pennsylvania Law Review* 105 (1957): 436.

New Brunswick. Accounting of Constables by Parish, 1805. Governmental Collection, New Brunswick Museum Archives, S181 F107.4(a).

____. An Act for the Appointment of Town and Parish Officers, in the several Counties of this Province. S.N.B. 26 Geo III (1786), c. 28, 1786. Reprinted in *Acts of the General Assembly of Her Majesty's Province of New Brunswick from the Twenty Sixth Year of the Reign of King George the Third to the Sixth Year of the Reign of King William the Fourth*, edited by George F.S. Berton. Fredericton, NB: John Simpson, Queen's Publisher, 1838.

____. Census (abridged) of Nova Scotia/New Brunswick, 1770. Available online: http://www.rootsweb.ancestry.com/~canns/nscensus1770. html?cj=1&netid=cj&o_xid=0001231185&o_lid=0001231185; accessed March 1, 2012.

____. Census of Sackville New Brunswick, 1820. Available online: http://www. rootsweb.ancestry.com/~nbwestmo/cen1820.htm; accessed April 2, 2012.

____. Census of Shediac Area, 1820. Provincial Archives of New Brunswick, microfilm F859.

____. Census returns, Westmorland County (1820/1824). Provincial Archives of New Brunswick, F859.

____. *Christian Steeves v. Jacob Peck*, 1823. Supreme Court Original Jurisdiction Records, 1784-1836. Provincial Archives of New Brunswick, RS42.

____. Commission appointing Ward Chipman Sr. as Judge of Supreme Court, 1809. New Brunswick Museum Archives, OS F21.1.

____. Costs due to the Clerk of the Crown on the Circuits from the County of Westmorland, June 1809. Hugh T. Hazen Collection, New Brunswick Museum Archives, F100.9.

____. Court documents re: Babcock (murder), 1805. Governmental Collection, New Brunswick Museum Archives, S181 F107.

____. Court documents re: Jerome (theft), 1805. Governmental Collection, New Brunswick Museum Archives, S181 F108.

____. Court documents re: Peck (blasphemy), 1805. Governmental Collection, New Brunswick Museum Archives, S181 F109.

____. *The Crown v. Luke Hamilton*, 1799. Hugh T. Hazen Collection, New Brunswick Museum Archives, S 65 F92. 16 (1).

____. Deed — Christian Steeves to James Watson, 1807. Governmental Collection, New Brunswick Museum Archives, S180 F57.16.

____. Hillsborough — General Return of Families, 1783. Colonial Office of Nova Scotia and Cape Breton. Co. 217, vol. 59 f 112.

____. *The King against Amos Babcock*, indictment for murder, 1805. Governmental Collection, New Brunswick Museum Archives, S181 F107.3.

____. Land grant of 222 acres to Robert Keillor in Westmorland County, October 16, 1786. Provincial Archives of New Brunswick, F16300.

____. Legal precepts — Westmorland County to the Sheriff, 1805. Governmental Collection, New Brunswick Museum Archives, OS F55.4.

____. List of Constables by Parish, 1805. Governmental Collection, New Brunswick Museum Archives, F107.4(d).

____. List of Petit jurors, June term, Dorchester Courthouse, 1805. Governmental Collection, New Brunswick Museum Archives, S181 F107.4.

____. List of Prisoners Confined in the Gaol at Parr Town, January 17, 1785. New Brunswick Museum Archives, S65 F96.1.

____. Minutes of the Supreme Court, 1785-1829. Loyalist Collection, Harriet Irving Library, LPR.N4C6S9M5, reel 1.

____. Mortgage deed — Peter Casey to John Atkinson, 1803. Governmental Collection, New Brunswick Museum Archives, S180 F48.8.

____. Muster rolls of Loyalist troops — Queen's Rangers, 1780 (Nelson and Harboard). New Brunswick Museum Archives, S26 F6 VI.

____. New Brunswick Executive Council: Treasurer's Accounts and Estimates, 1787-1851, 1851. Loyalist Collection, Harriet Irving Library, FC LPR. N4E9T7.

____. New Brunswick Historical Society Fonds, 1874-1969. New Brunswick Museum Archives, S25-29 F1-303.

____. New Brunswick Land Records for Westmorland County: Deeds, Mortgages and Leases, 1767-1853. Loyalist Collection, Harriet Irving Library, FC LPR.N4L3W5D4.

____. Ordinance for establishing the Supreme Court of New Brunswick, 1784. Hugh T. Hazen Collection, New Brunswick Museum Archives, S64 F59.22.

____. Record of the Minutes of the Proceedings of the Courts of Nisi Prius, Oyer and Terminer and Gaol Delivery of the Province of New Brunswick for the year 1786 to 1808. Provincial Archives of New Brunswick, RS36 A1.

____. Records of the Court of General Sessions of the Peace — Sunbury County, 1782-1825. Provincial Archives of New Brunswick, RS157.

____. Supreme Court Records, 1785-1834. Harriet Irving Library, Loyalist Collection, LPR.N4C6S9R4.

____. 1883. Westmorland Local Records, 1751-1883. Loyalist Collection, Harriet Irving Library, LPR.N4P8W4L6.

____. Westmorland Marriage Registry, 1790-1835. Loyalist Collection, Harriet Irving Library, FC LPR.N4C6S4W4M3R4.

____. Westmorland Probate Court Records, 2 v., 1787-1843, and 1787-1839. Loyalist Collection, Harriet Irving Library, FC LPR.N4C6P7W4R4.

____. Westmorland Cemetery Records. James Humphrey Collection, Provincial Archives of New Brunswick, MC600 MS4 A and C.

New Brunswick Courier. "Obituary of William Botsford," May 14, 1864. Provincial Archives of New Brunswick, Daniel F. John's New Brunswick Newspaper Vital Statistics Database, vol. 22, no. 94, rank 76.

New Brunswick Reporter and Fredricton Advertiser. "100th anniversary of Botsford landing," November 28, 1882. Provincial Archives of New Brunswick, Daniel F. John's New Brunswick Newspaper Vital Statistics Database, vol. 58, no. 1716, rank 152.

New Brunswick Royal Gazette. "Estate notice — Amos Botsford," March 22, 1813. Provincial Archives of New Brunswick, Daniel F. John's New Brunswick Newspaper Vital Statistics Database, vol. 1, no. 1351, rank 101.

____. "Obituary — Amos Botsford," September 21, 1812. Provincial Archives of New Brunswick, Daniel F. John's New Brunswick Newspaper Vital Statistics Database, vol. 1, no. 1308, rank 101.

Nickerson, Thomas. Land grant petition in Westmorland (with Amasa Killam), 1806. Provincial Archives of New Brunswick, RS108 Index of Land Petitions, 1783-1918, F4171.

Nova Scotia. *The Crown v. Mosely,* 1784. Commissioner of Public Records Collection, Nova Scotia Archives, 1702-1917, Special Subjects, 1729-1867, RG1 vol. 341-396.

____. Marriage registry (Abner Hall and Mercy Babcock), December 17, 1772. Nova Scotia Archives, Cornwallis Township Records, 1720-1874, MFM 12261.

____. Record of Births for the Township of Cornwallis. Nova Scotia Archives, Cornwallis Township Records, 1720-1874, MFM 15031.

Olsson, Peter A. *Malignant Pied Pipers of Our Time: A Psychological Study of Destructive Cult Leaders from Rev. Jim Jones to Osama Bin Laden.* Baltimore: Publish America, 2005.

Palatine Project. "List of German Passengers aboard the Pearl, 1751." Available online: http://www.progenealogists.com/palproject/ns/1751pearl.htm; accessed March 1, 2012.

Palmer, Gideon. Findings of the coroner's inquest (Mercy Hall), February 20, 1805. Governmental Collection, New Brunswick Museum Archives, OS F55.8.

____. Inquest — Park Davison, 1808. Hugh T. Hazen Collection, New Brunswick Museum Archives, S65 F90.11.

____. Land grant #86, awarding 245 acres in Memramcook River to Palmer, October 16, 1786. Provincial Archives of New Brunswick, F16300.

____. Letter to Amos Botsford of Fredericton, February 20, 1805. Governmental Collection, New Brunswick Museum Archives, S181 F107.1.

Peck, Jacob. Marriage Bond to Joyce Alrod, December 10, 1804. New Brunswick Museum Archives, Westmorland County Marriage Bonds, 1798-1811, S89-2 F57.65.

____. Petition for a land grant in Hillsborough County, 1791. Provincial Archives of New Brunswick, RS108 Index of Land Petitions, 1783-1918, F1038.

Peck, Martin Sr. Land Grant #180, 237 acres in Hillsborough Parish,

Westmorland, February 12, 1789. Provincial Archives of New Brunswick, New Brunswick Land Grants, 1784-1997, F16300.

____. Land Grant # 121, 500 acres in Cumberland Township, 1786. Provincial Archives of New Brunswick, New Brunswick Land Grants, 1784-1997, F16302.

Pennington, Kenneth. "Innocent until Proven Guilty: The Origins of a Legal Maxim." *Jurist* 63 (2003): 106-124.

Pilon, Marilyn. "Mental Disorder and Canadian Criminal Law." Law and Government Division publication PRB 99 — 22E. Ottawa: Library of Parliament, Parliamentary Research Branch, October 5, 1999; rev. January 22, 2002. Available online: http://publications.gc.ca/collections/Collection-R/LoPBdP/BP/prb9922-e.htm; accessed February 22, 2012.

Puddington, I.E. "The History of the Canadian Society of Forensic Science." *Journal of the Canadian Society of Forensic Science* 11, no. 2 (1978). Available online: http://www.csfs.ca/eng/history/the-history-of-the-canadian-society-of-forensic-science; accessed February 22, 2012.

Rawlyk, George A. *Ravished by the Spirit: Religious Revivals, Baptists and Henry Alline*. Kingston, ON: Queen's University Press, 1984.

Raymond, W.O. *Winslow Papers, 1776-1826*. Saint John, NB: Sun Printing Company, 1901.

Rembar, Charles. *The Law of the Land*. New York: Simon & Schuster, 1980.

Reynolds, William ["Roslynde," pseud.]. "The Babcock Tragedy." *New Brunswick Magazine* 1 (July 1898): 214-222. Available on microfiche at the Provincial Archives of New Brunswick or online: http://archive.org/stream/newbrunswickmaga01stjouoft/newbrunswickmaga01stjouoft_djvu.txt.

____. Invoice to R.R. Stock, March 8, 1878. W.K. Reynolds Collection, New Brunswick Museum Archive, CB DOC item 9.

Royal Canadian Mounted Police. "The RCMP's History." Available online: http://www.rcmp-grc.gc.ca/hist/index-eng.htm; accessed February 22, 2012.

Royal Gazette. "Trial of Amos Babcock," June 26, 1805. Newspaper Collection, Provincial Archives of New Brunswick.

Saint John Daily Sun. "Obituary of Joseph W. Lawrence," November 7, 1892. Provincial Archives of New Brunswick, Daniel F. John's New Brunswick Newspaper Vital Statistics Database, vol. 85, no. 1033, rank 182.

Saint John Daily Telegraph. "Christian Steeves of Hillsborough," October 22, 1884. Provincial Archives of New Brunswick, Daniel F. John's New Brunswick Newspaper Vital Statistics Database, vol. 61, no. 2638, rank 101.

Saint John Gazette. "Guilty verdict in Amos Babcock trial," June 24, 1805. Provincial Archives of New Brunswick, Daniel F. John's New Brunswick Newspaper Vital Statistics Database, vo. 1, no. 685, rank 101.

Saint John Globe. "Gideon Palmer obituary," July 2, 1880. Provincial Archives of New Brunswick, Daniel F. John's New Brunswick Newspaper Vital Statistics Database, vol. 52, no. 2237, rank 76.

Sands, Edward. Coroner's inquest of Elsey "Alice" West, rape and murder by Luke Hamilton, August 8, 1799. Hugh T. Hazen Collection, New Brunswick Museum Archives, S 65 F90.7.

Scott, Robert. Petition for a land grant in Salisbury Parish (includes Jacob Peck), July 24, 1810. Provincial Archives of New Brunswick, RS108 Index of Land Petitions, 1783-1918, F4174.

Shoebottom, Bradley T. "The Nova Scotia 1767 and 1770-87 Census and the Westmorland Census of 1803 and 1820." Available online: http://rmc-ca. academia.edu/BradleyShoebottom/Papers/89843/The_Nova_Scotia_1767_ and_1770-87_Census_and_the_Westmorland_New_Brunswick_Census_ of_1803_and_1820; accessed March 2, 2012.

Soucoup, Dan. *Historic New Brunswick*. Lawrencetown, NS: Pottersfield Press, 1997.

Taylor, George. *A History of Salisbury, 1774-1984, with Notes on the Acadian and Pre-European Periods*. Salisbury, NB: Bicentennial Commission of New Brunswick, Salisbury Committee, 1984.

Taylor, Greg. *Law of the Land: The Advent of the Torrens System in Canada*. Toronto: University of Toronto Press, 2008.

Tibbedou, Germain. Petition for a land grant in Westmorland County, 1786. Provincial Archives of New Brunswick, RS108 Index of Land Grant Petitions, 1783-1918, F1032.

Underwood, John. Petition for a land grant in Westmorland County, 1808. Provincial Archives of New Brunswick, RS108 Index of Land Grants, 1783-1918, F4172.

United Empire Loyalists' Association of Canada. "Loyalist Genealogy of John Welling II." Available online: http://www.uelac.org/Loyalist-Info/extras/ Welling-John/Welling-John-biography.php; accessed March 31, 2012.

United States. January 4, 1892. *Commonwealth v. Randolph (Pennsylvania)*. Available online: http://www.outhistory.org/wiki/index. php?title=Commonwealth_v._Randolph_(Pennsylvania):_January_4,_189 2&diff=40554&oldid=prev; accessed April 2, 2012.

Upham, Joshua. Land grant for Joshua Upham, Burton Parish, 1786. Provincial Archives of New Brunswick, RS108 Index of Land Grants, 1783-1918, F16300.

____. Land grant for Joshua Upham, Carleton Township, 1785. Provincial Archives of New Brunswick, RS108 Index of Land Grants, 1783-1918, F16302.

____. Letter to Edward Winslow, August 27, 1783. University of New Brunswick Library, MG H2.

____. Letter to George Duncan Ludlow, [n.d.]. Hugh T. Hazen Collection, New Brunswick Museum Archives, F96-6.

____. Letter to Henry Knox, December 1, 1783. Henry Knox Collection, Massachusetts Historical Society.

____. Letter to Timothy Pickering, November 18, 1783. Library and Archives Canada, MG 23, D1 ser.l.4: 1318-21.

____. Letter to Ward Chipman regarding the application of New Brunswick judges, 1808. Hugh T. Hazen Colllection, New Brunswick Museum Archives, S38-1 F20.7.

Walker, David A. "Ancestral Trails — Biography of Gideon Palmer." Available online: http://www.ancestraltrails.ca/walker%20for%20web-o/p732. htm#i268; accessed January 25, 2012.

Watson, James. Release of Jacob Peck on his own recognizances, February 25, 1805. Governmental Collection, New Brunswick Museum Archives, S 181 F109.3.

Webster, John Clarence. *A History of Shediac, New Brunswick.* Privately printed, 1928. Reprinted, Saint John: New Brunswick Museum, 1953.

Webster, John Clarence. Notes re: William Hanington, [n.d.]. William Lusk Webster Collection, New Brunswick Museum Archives, S204-1 F6-3.

____. Specifications for various houses (early 1800s), [n.d.]. William Lusk Webster Collection, New Brunswick Museum Archives, S204-1 F11.

Webster, John Clarence, and J.R. Bourque. Notes re: early English period (Shediac), [n.d.]. William Lusk Webster Collection, New Brunswick Museum Archives, S204-1 F6.

Welling, John. Land grant # 435 — 193 acres in Shediac to John Welling, 1806. Provincial Archives of New Brunswick, F16303.

Yogis, John A., ed. *Barron's Canadian Law Dictionary*, 4th ed. Hauppauge, NY: Barron's Educational, 2003.

Additional Archival Sources

Babcock Family History notes. Provincial Archives of New Brunswick, MC600 MS1A2.

Benedict Arnold Papers, 1741-1801. New Brunswick Museum Archives, S 29 C.

Benedict Arnold and Monson Hayt Fonds, University of New Brunswick Archives, MG H3 F1-7.

Biography of William Hanington. Provincial Archives of New Brunswick, MC1286, vol. VII.

Botsford family history — William Botsford's accounts. Botsford Family Collection, New Brunswick Museum Archives, S123-1.

Hanington family history. Hanington Family Fonds, New Brunswick Museum Archives, 0.5 CB DOC.1.

Joseph W. Lawrence Collection, 1818-1892. New Brunswick Museum Archives, S14 A76, S17 A313.

William Obder Raymond Collection, 1853-1923. New Brunswick Museum Archives, S98-S98A.

William Reynolds Collection, 1865-1887. New Brunswick Museum Archives, CB DOC.

Illustration Credits

The lyrics from "The Ballad of Jacob Peck" by John Bottomley on page 7 appear courtesy of the Estate of John Bottomley. The following signatures appear courtesy of the Provincial Archives of New Brunswick: Jacob Peck, pg. 23 (F1038); Amos Babcock, pg. 35 (F1043); Jonathon Babcock, pg. 75 (F1043); Leonard Peck, pg. 141 (F4174) and Jacob Peck, pg. 201 (F4174). The following signatures appear courtesy of the New Brunswick Museum, Saint John, NB: Jacob Peck, pg. 27 (S89-2 F57.65); William Hanington, pg. 43 (Governmental Collection, S181 F107.2); Mary Hanington, pg. 59 (Governmental Collection, S181 F107.2); John Welling, pg. 67 (Governmental Collection, S181 F107.2); William Kilby Reynolds, pg. 99 (William Reynolds Collection, CB DOC, item 9); Amasa Killam, pg. 105 (Governmental Collection, S181 F107.2); Gideon Palmer, pg. 115 (OS F55.1); Amos Botsford, pg. 129 (Hugh T. Hazen Collection, S65 F100.15); William Botsford, pg. 129 (Governmental Collection S181 F80.2); Jonathon Babcock, pg. 145 (Governmental Collection, S181 F107.2); Joshua Upham, pg. 149, (F96.6); Ward Chipman, pg. 161 (S36 F11.11) and John Jerome, pg. 189 (Governmental Collection, S181 F108.1). The signature of Robert Keillor on page 111 (Trueman Family Fonds, Reference no. 0102/1/9) appears courtesy of the Mount Allison University Archives. All lyrics and illustrative material are reproduced with permission.

Index

DEBRA KOMAR earned a PhD from the University of Alberta and was a tenured associate professor at the University of New Mexico. A Fellow of the American Academy of Forensic Sciences and a practicing forensic anthropologist for over twenty years, she has investigated human rights violations for the United Nations and Physicians for Human Rights, testifying as an expert witness in The Hague and across North America.